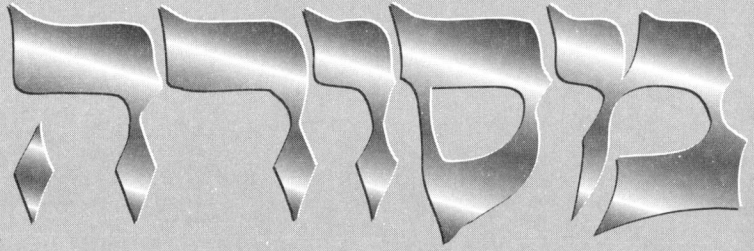

ArtScroll Series®

Rabbi Nosson Scherman / Rabbi Meir Zlotowitz
General Editors

A Mother's

by
Sheina Medwed

Published by
Mesorah Publications, ltd

Favorite Stories

FIRST EDITION
First Impression ... November 1998

Published and Distributed by
MESORAH PUBLICATIONS, LTD.
4401 Second Avenue / Brooklyn, N.Y 11232

Distributed in Europe by
J. LEHMANN HEBREW BOOKSELLERS
20 Cambridge Terrace
Gateshead, Tyne and Wear
England NE8 1RP

Distributed in Israel by
SIFRIATI / A. GITLER
10 Hashomer Street
Bnei Brak 51361

Distributed in Australia and New Zealand by
GOLDS BOOK & GIFT SHOP
36 William Street
Balaclava 3183, Vic., Australia

Distributed in South Africa by
KOLLEL BOOKSHOP
Shop 8A Norwood Hypermarket
Norwood 2196, Johannesburg, South Africa

ARTSCROLL SERIES®
A MOTHER'S FAVORITE STORIES
© Copyright 1998, by MESORAH PUBLICATIONS, Ltd.
4401 Second Avenue / Brooklyn, N.Y. 11232 / (718) 921-9000

ALL RIGHTS RESERVED
The text, prefatory and associated textual contents and introductions
— including the typographic layout, cover artwork and ornamental graphics —
have been designed, edited and revised as to content, form and style.

No part of this book may be reproduced
IN ANY FORM, PHOTOCOPING, OR COMPUTER RETRIEVAL SYSTEMS
— even for personal use without written permission from
the copyright holder, Mesorah Publications Ltd.
except by a reviewer who wishes to quote brief passages
in connection with a review written for inclusion in magazines or newspapers.

THE RIGHTS OF THE COPYRIGHT HOLDER WILL BE STRICTLY ENFORCED.

ISBN:
1-57819-298-6 (hard cover)
1-57819-299-4 (paperback)

Typography by Compuscribe at ArtScroll Studios, Ltd.
4401 Second Avenue / Brooklyn, N.Y. 11232 / (718) 921-9000

Printed in the United States of America by Moriah Offset
Bound by Sefercraft, Quality Bookbinders, Ltd. Brooklyn, N.Y.

Dedicated
in memory of
my father,
Asher Ben Mordechai,
of blessed memory,
whose life embodied simplicity and humility;

and in honor of
my mother,
Rochel Kempner תחי׳,
whose sincere faith and optimism radiates to all.

Table of Contents

Introduction	9
Acknowledgments	15
Choices	21
Torah Values	51
For the Sake of Peace	93
Saving Lives	105
Modesty	135
Nature's Bounty	151
Kindness	167
Partners in Life	201
Epilogue	253

Introduction

"My son, hear the instruction of your father, and do not forsake the Torah of your mother." (Proverbs 1:8)

The winter of 1986 in Jerusalem was cold and rainy. As I walked home from a class in seminary, I had a vague sense of uneasiness. It wasn't the loneliness I sometimes felt at being so far from family, nor was it related to the culture shock of being in a new country. It went deeper.

It was a kind of loneliness I couldn't explain or define.

No matter how much I missed my family, I took comfort in the fact that my husband and I were privileged to be in Jerusalem learning Torah. My teachers were brilliant and friendly, our neighbors all wonderful people.

So what was bothering me?

Like a bolt of lightning, a dual realization struck me.

The first part of this insight was that I missed my Bubbie, which seemed bizarre, since I never really knew her. She passed away when I was an infant. How could I miss someone I never knew?

The second part of the realization came in the form of questions: Who really taught me about G–d? Who was instrumental in teaching me that He runs the world and that I have a direct and personal relationship with Him?

Deep inside, I know He is with me no matter what. At any given moment, all I have to do is remember Him and I have restored my connection. Whether I am walking or cooking or folding laundry, reading or visiting with a friend, the opportunity to be connected to and aware of my

Creator is always there. He is not hidden in a book; He is everywhere.

Who taught you this? I asked myself over and over as I walked along that cold afternoon. And then, with the clarity and freshness of rain, I knew.

It was my mother. She was my first teacher. My mother had taught me about G-d — not through texts or lectures, but through her very being.

❧ My Mother, My First Teacher

"Look, sweetheart — look how the grass pushes through the sidewalk! See how G–d makes things grow? Would you ever think a tiny blade of grass could do such a thing, grow like that right through the pavement?"

We were walking along the sidewalks of the Bronx, my three-year-old hand tucked inside her coat pocket, my head turned down toward the gray cement. Sure enough, there was a long green blade of grass with tiny baby blades sprouting through the sidewalk. It didn't make sense. How could the soft tender grass push through concrete?

Glimpses of truth — of the extraordinary work of Hashem hidden in the details of everyday life — were part of my growing up. It was not so much a conscious instruction, but something that sprang forth from the wellspring of my mother's being. She recognized the majesty of her Creator in every little thing. While walking the city blocks on ordinary errands or going for a Sunday afternoon ride on the Cross-Bronx Expressway, she sang the praises of all the green miracles along the way. "Look how the grass grows through the pavement, how the trees root themselves despite the bedrock stone!"

Digging into the recesses of childhood memories, I hear the chirping of Willie, our blue parakeet. My mother stands by his cage with her right hand inside, a ready, patient perch. She holds it steady, waiting for the bird to trust her. As she holds it there, she talks in bird language interspersed with bird English, "Come uppie to Ma, come uppie to Ma, such a pretty birdie, such a pretty birdie." I watch in timid fascination, wondering what softness would be discovered by touching those blue underbelly feathers that were so close to my mother's extended finger.

The Bronx sparrows and pigeons that adorned our apartment windowsill were always rewarded with bread crumbs and sunflower seeds, as well as a whistle-song and a bit of conversation. In our house, even an orange seed sprouting within its fruit was cause for celebration. "Look how G-d makes things grow!" The seed would be put aside in a glass of water to be nurtured and cherished and eventually planted in its own pot of soil. We had quite a few orange plants on various sills, each one a testimony to my mother's love of life. Little did I know back then that my mother, by the very nature of her being, was planting within me a deep appreciation for the beauty and holiness of all life.

My mother was my first teacher. My mother taught me about G-d — not through texts, not through lectures, but through her very being. Through her being she transmitted something that Western culture could not touch, that foreign ideologies could never tarnish. How I watched her stand, utterly still, whispering her prayers, her *neshamah* aflame like the Shabbos candles. How she sang Yiddish lullabies that sank their notes deep into the fibers of my heart!

This is how I learned about Hashem. Right there on the Jerusalem sidewalk, right through the beige-golden stone, the green leaves were growing, thriving, and flowering.

How could something tender and green root itself in the bedrock stone and flourish there? With her enthusiasm for all things green and living, my mother had planted within me both an awareness of Hashem and a paradigm for my inner struggles, a personal metaphor that whispers over and over, "Grow! Take root! Push through!"

And as I walked home that day in the late afternoon rain of Jerusalem, my uneasiness was replaced by longing — longing to know what it meant, really meant, to be a Jewish woman. What does it mean to build a Jewish home?

I knew that learning was vitally important, but I had a sense deep in my intuitive being that there was another scroll I needed, an invisible one. It was a scroll whose words had for generations been imperceptibly printed in the atmosphere of a true Jewish home. I wouldn't find it on the bookshelves of the seminary. The book I needed to read was written on the inner scroll of my Bubbie's heart.

It was a distinctly woman's book, inscribed in the hearts and beings of Jewish women from the inception of our people. My Bubbie carried this scroll from Minsk to Massachusetts. My mother bore it inside herself in the Springfield public schools. Now I had come to Jerusalem to "learn" it. Yet it wasn't something that could be read like a text. I had no book; I had no commentaries. All I had was a longing in my heart resonating something essential from within my being. Something that pulsated beyond culture, beyond language — like the tiny blade of grass pushing its way through the rock — to find the core of my soul.

What does it mean to be a Jewish woman? What does it mean in terms of personal life? And what does it mean in terms of history?

Every Jewish woman is a link in a chain that goes back through time to the tent of our Mother Sarah. We can follow this chain through the fields of Egypt where the women cooked fish for their exhausted husbands; into the desert where, in the merit of Miriam the Prophetess, who taught Torah to the women, we had water for 40 years. We can see how Naomi carried this chain into the fields of Moav to return with Ruth, who lived to sit on a special royal throne next to her great-great-grandson, King Solomon; and how, in the hands of Esther, this chain was drawn through the corridors of Ahasuerus' palace. We look from afar at how the Greeks and Romans used every ounce of strength and cunning to sever the links in our chain, yet we emerged again in the Torah centers of Europe and the Mediterranean, only to journey forward once again, downtrodden but singing, in the dust of the Spanish expulsion. We can follow this chain's progress through concentration camps, see it lying in the forests where the women hid in trenches, and watch as women walked into the icy Russian rivers with this chain in their hearts, and marched into the gas chambers, pure and untouched.

When Jewish women went forward with nothing to hold onto — no food to feed their family, no home, nothing except the sky and earth and air to sustain them — they trudged along with a link in their hands.

We ask ourselves, as did women in times past, "What does Hashem want from us? In what way am I a link in this eternal chain?"

It is my hope and prayer that the stories you read here will add to your appreciation, as they did to mine, of the greatness of Jewish women everywhere.

I think back to a scene that took place two days before we made *aliyah* — I am at my parents' home. The living room is filled with shopping bags, boxes and suitcases. After our morning cup of coffee, I follow my mother around the house like a baby duckling, trying to memorize everything about her: the rhythm of her actions, how she moves papers from one room to the next, how she talks to herself in her fiery alto voice, "Now Rosie, you must remember to call … and you must write your niece a letter … and this week is your granddaughter's birthday … where is that card …"

I am frozen by the fact that two days later, I will be 6,000 miles away from her, starting a new life with my husband. Suddenly I put my arms around her and say, "Mama, I'm going to miss you so much."

"Oh, sweetheart," she says, "I'm so sad."

And there we were, crying in the middle of the living room in the Bronx.

Now I find myself wondering, "How did my Bubbie feel?" She stepped onto a boat to sail to America and I stepped onto an El Al jet to leave America and come to Jerusalem. Jewish women, mothers and daughters, leaving and being left, moving with the ocean and the air currents of history.

How much cooking and cleaning and scrubbing and changing, inspiring, sewing, ironing, coordinating, *chesed*, baking and disciplining is packed into the cycle of just one day in the life of a Jewish woman. Spinning with exhaustion, woken up in mid-sleep, how difficult it is at times to see past the clock into a vision of history and purpose.

Yet there are moments that lift us up above the routine into the eternal.

What was my Bubbie's life like? I wonder. What collection of moments forged her links in the unbroken chain? What about the lives of other Jewish women in recent history? How did they transmit the living Torah?

As I walked home in the cold Jerusalem rain, I knew that this was the scroll I now needed to study.

Acknowledgments

With a heart full of gratitude to the One Who is the source of all blessing and creativity, I give thanks to Hashem who has given me the privilege of using His gifts to write this book.

From an early age, my mother, Mrs. Rose Kempner, may she live and be well, instilled within me a love for people and their stories. In that sense, this book is hers as well.

I am indebted to the many fascinating and inspiring people who were kind enough to share their stories with me. Some of them wish to remain anonymous. The others are mentioned directly with their stories. I thank all of you profusely for the contribution you made to this project and the enriching impact that you have had on my personal life.

There are people who gave me indispensable guidance and direction in clarifying the underlying theme of this book. Rebbetzin Denah Weinberg and Rebbetzin Yitty Neustadt have been instrumental in helping me have a deeper understanding of the concept of *"Toras Imecha"* and how it relates to the challenges for the contemporary Jewish woman and her home.

There are people who demonstrated their support by directing me to sources of stories. In particular I would like to thank HaRav Shlomo Ashkenazi, Rabbi Mordechai Perlman, Rabbi Benzion Ezrachi, Rabbi Shlomo Fishman, Rabbi Yaakov Bear on behalf of HaRav Moshe Sternbuch, Rebbetzin Chaya Heyman and Mrs. Rina Orloweck.

There are people who gave me invaluable assistance in gathering the material for this book. Mrs. Debbie Goldberg conducted interviews; Esther Leah Lewin conducted interviews and translated a letter from Yiddish to English. My dear friend Mrs. Lily Yachnes spoke with me for hours at a time when the book was in its very beginning stages. She conducted interviews in Hebrew and then translated them into English, thus enabling me to have access to those with whom I otherwise would not have been fortunate enough to communicate. Mrs. Ruth Pepperman painstakingly and quickly transcribed many taped interviews, often expressing delight, interest and curiosity about the material.

During the course of this project I have learned the importance of words of encouragement. To the many kind neighbors and friends in Har Nof and other communities of Jerusalem, I wish to extend my heartfelt appreciation for their thoughtful words of support. There were times of intense work when my contact with the outside world took place in the aisles of the supermarket. These messengers of encouragement have no idea how much their words meant.

In particular, my friend Mrs. Shulamis Tilles, a founding member of Ascent Institute, read parts of the manuscript, inspired me with her enthusiasm and helped me find stories. Mrs. Chaya Heller, the founder and director of Beit Natan, expressed a high level of excitement for the project. Our cousins Eliezer and Sarah Medwed expressed genuine interest and concern for the completion of the project. My debt of gratitude also extends to all my fellow participants in the relaxation seminar led by Dr. Gary Quinn and Dr. Aryeh Mishkin, who helped me, in a uniquely creative way, to clarify priorities in order to successfully meet the deadlines for the book.

In both the creative and technical preparation of this

book, I have been extremely privileged to be part of a team whose experience and professionalism are superlative. Reb Shmuel Blitz of Artscroll, Jerusalem gave form and structure to an idea that I had been trying to formalize for years. This book could not have been written without his clear direction and guidance. My editor, Mrs. Aviva Rappaport, used her combined expertise as both a technician and an artist to shape and polish these stories. Her understanding of the role of the Jewish woman and the fundamental importance of the home permeates the inner structure of this book. Devora Rhein's editorial comments were extremely appreciated and useful.

I have been blessed with a typist who, as well as being a dear friend, is also an avid and critical reader. Her eye for language would allow nothing to pass on her computer screen if it didn't sound right. Mrs. Aviva Zweig has worked with me since the very beginning of this project. She has often, at the last minute, changed her schedule so that we could sit together and meet a deadline. She has been a constant source of skillful help and encouragement.

In Hebrew there is an expression, אַחֲרוֹן אַחֲרוֹן חָבִיב, meaning the last is the most precious. It is with this in mind that I thank my husband, Dr. Zalman Medwed, D.C., and our son Yitzchak Meir, for their devotion to *"Ima's* book."

It is personally significant that the writing was finished during the early part of the week following *Parashas Ki Savo*, which has in it the mitzvah of *bikkurim*, the first fruits. This is a first book. In the *Mussaf* of the three festivals we pray: "We should not appear before Hashem emptyhanded, but each according to the gift Hashem placed in his hand." With this in mind, *bli neder*, I dedicate the *ma'aser* from this book to Talmud Torah Ahavas Torah HaMesorah, a *cheder* whose standards of excellence will, *b'ezras Hashem,* continue to bear fruit that will carry the sweetness of Torah into future generations.

The Sforno tells us that every prayer is incomplete without the remembrance of Jerusalem (*Psalms* 137:6). Therefore with the prayer that these stories strengthen and inspire all of us to cleave to that which is holy and pure in the creation of our homes and families, let us pray to see the restoration of Hashem's home, the rebuilding of Yerushalayim, *Ir HaKodesh,* and the coming of *Mashiach,* speedily in our days, Amen.

Sheina Medwed
Har Nof, Jerusalem
Rosh Chodesh Cheshvan 5759

A Mother's Favorite Stories

Choices

✺ She Couldn't ... She Just Couldn't

The scene: Shabbos, just after candlelighting. Sophie is holding her youngest grandchild in her arms and singing to her. "Maidele, a gutten Shabbos, maidele, that's right, you are a bas melech, a daughter of the King ..." The baby's eyes seem to follow the silken lilting sound.

How many generations of love and mesiras nefesh (self-sacrifice) are being poured into this tiny granddaughter's being as the flames of the Shabbos candles bear witness! And who knows when this child, as she grows, will call upon inner resources from this moment in time? Who knows when she will make choices which will resound with the strength of her Bubbie's message?

From grandmother to granddaughter — from where had Sophie drawn her unshakable faith? Only years later would this granddaughter know her story ...

It was wartime in Russia, and the Gelbsteins had nothing to eat. However, Sophie, their 12-year-old daughter, offered them hope. She sewed quickly and she sewed well, and factories were working round-the-clock, seven days a week, to provide uniforms for the soldiers. Maybe she could find a job.

She began working on a Sunday and worked throughout the week, producing more garments than anyone else.

Then came that first Shabbos. She did not even know for

what to *daven*. How could she *daven* to keep her job if it meant working on Shabbos? Yet how could she *daven* to lose it, knowing the family would have nothing to eat? She walked to work without carrying anything.

It was late when she arrived at the factory. Everyone was watching her as she walked toward the sewing machine. They all knew she was the Rabbi's daughter. She sat down at the machine and stared at the threads, the needles, the large metal scissors that cut through layers of thick fabric. Her hands were cold and shaking and her face was burning from embarrassment.

She sat still and waited. All of a sudden she saw the factory manager coming towards her with her right fist raised high in the air. "You traitor!" she screamed, "I'll make sure you lose this job and any other sewing job around!"

Although considered very mature for her age, Sophie burst into tears. She thought of Shabbos at home, the sound of her father's *davening,* the candles flickering, and the singing. She thought of praying alongside her mother next to the warm charcoal stove on Shabbos morning. Then she thought of the *Sefer Torah* in the plain wooden closet that stood in their living room. This was the Torah that her father had saved when the *shul* had caught on fire. Since then, the village *minyan* (quorum of ten) met in their home. They couldn't think of rebuilding the *shul* when there wasn't even enough money for bread.

She was hungry from her long walk and dizzy from crying. She knew that saving a life took priority over Shabbos. Wasn't money for food considered saving a life? She tried to touch the scissors, but her hand wouldn't move. "What can I do besides sew?" she wondered. "How will we eat?"

And then, it was as though her parents were standing

beside her. She imagined her father's hands on her head as he blessed her every Friday night, and she heard him whisper as he always did afterwards, "You are a daughter of the King, my precious one, a daughter of the King."

"No," she screamed inside herself, "the King's daughter doesn't work on Shabbos. Food comes from G–d, not the Russian government!" She raised her head and looked around. Somehow the manager had gone back to her post, and her comrades were busy working and chattering. No one had beat her. No one had fired her.

She breathed a sigh of relief and recited the morning prayers.

Years later, Sophie told her children that every Shabbos it was the same. The manager would scream and threaten, all eyes would be fixed on her, and then within half an hour it was work as usual. Except for Sophie. Every Shabbos she just sat, head down on the sewing table next to her machine, and cried.

Looking Backward, Moving Forward

Gila Moskowitz, a teacher in a Hebrew Day Academy and a young mother of three, lives in the Southeast. In this story we see how a trip to Poland's death camps as a teenager forced her to take a good, hard look at her lifestyle and evaluate whether her commitment to Judaism was real or superficial. This vivid account of her very moving experience on the last day of the tour shows us how one young woman forced herself to wrestle head-on with the fact of the Holocaust, and what it meant personally for her life choices. Her turning point is a story that will be handed down in her family for generations to come.

It had been a difficult year for Gila. She felt as though she were caught between conflicting worlds. Her parents were modern Orthodox in their observance but very, very liberal in allowing her to make her own choices, especially when it came to school and friends. So, although she always went to Jewish day schools, she had a wide spectrum of friends. Sometimes when she came home from one of their social events she felt like she was living a schizophrenic life.

Now she stood at a major crossroads in her life. She had just received her letter of acceptance to a Teachers Academy. Going there meant a deeper commitment to a Jewish way of life. She was sure that it also meant losing some of her friends. She decided to postpone her decision. She requested a month's extension from the school and asked her parents if their offer to send her on a Jewish history tour of Poland was still feasible. The previous year when they had first mentioned it, she hadn't wanted to go, more out of fear than anything else. But now she felt that the trip might help her put her decision into perspective.

Gila stood at the entrance to an Auschwitz barracks. It was empty. The entrance was hidden by overgrown bushes, and a small window pane was covered with cobwebs and dust. It was the last day of her high-school tour of Poland and she still felt like her heart was a heart of stone. "What's wrong with me?" she thought. "I've stood in the actual gas chambers where the walls were scratched by the fingernails of dying Jews, and I haven't shed even one tear." While most of her friends were having a very emotional, tearful experience, she was beginning to wonder whether or not something was wrong with her. She kept trying to arouse her emotions, screaming inwardly, "Look where you are standing! Look at what you are seeing!" But try as she might, all she felt was a complete blank.

Even though she had been "touring" concentration camps for the last ten days, the fact that six million Jews had perished was something that had not yet moved Gila's heart. Yet, being the sensitive, thinking person she was, it was impossible for her to just shrug off the experience. She knew she had to break herself open to feeling. But how? She decided to wander off on her own, far away from the others in the group. Maybe then the experience would have more of an impact.

She walked through the mid-afternoon summer air, past barrack after barrack, until she found one almost totally covered by a tangle of vines. She felt sure that no one else would go in there. Scared, but determined to jolt herself awake emotionally, she pulled some of the growth away from the door and walked in.

Inside, the air was hazy with thick dust. Dirt was everywhere. Layers of decades-old dust covered the beds, where bits of straw and decaying blankets still lay. Cobwebs hung from the ceiling and clung to the walls. Dim light filtered in through the tiny cracked window. Gila stood there in silence, taking in the scene in front of her, trying to imagine this prison that she had forced herself to enter as it had been 50 years ago, full of Jews. But no — she stopped herself — it was more than that. "It wasn't full of

Jews, Gila," she said to herself. "That's just a cliché. It was filled with *people*. Each and every person who was killed was a whole world. Mothers and fathers and sons and daughters and aunts and uncles. Think of your own family. Think of all the generations of people who were never even born because their mothers and fathers died here."

Just as she was beginning to feel a tiny stirring in her heart, she heard the door open behind her. "Oh, no," she thought, "someone else is in here." She turned around and, sure enough, a friend from the tour had walked in and was equally surprised to see Gila standing there. They had both come for the same reason: to be alone. They stood there, saying nothing.

All of a sudden, a loud crash of glass broke the silence. They both froze for an instant and then ran out. The other girl was closest to the door, so she got out first. Once Gila was safely outside, though, she caught herself and said, "Don't you dare run away. You are running from the sound of glass shattering? The people who were here had to live and suffer in these very barracks with no escape. You go back in there and prove to yourself that it was nothing." She felt that if she ran away she would be rejecting her collective history as a Jew, her ability to somehow bring into her young heart a thread of connection with the people who had died there.

Shaking with fear, her hands cold, she reopened the door. She felt she had to prove to herself that what she had heard was not a ghost. She was walking around the barracks slowly when suddenly she heard another crash, this time not as loud. She followed the sound. It was coming from the far side of the barracks. Between two beds, a bottom bunk and a top bunk, there was a square window. She stood in front of it and saw a little baby bird. The bird was sitting on the window sill. The baby bird jumped up and hit the window and fell back down onto the window sill. Then it jumped up again and hit the window, and fell back onto the sill. She watched, fascinated by the stubborn persistence of this tiny bird. Then in one final attempt to get out, it jumped up, and flung itself with force against the window. The force of the blow repelled the bird and it fell backwards through a crack in the bed onto the floor.

Gila felt panic rising within her. She knelt down to look under the bed, but could not bring herself to reach through the thick net of cobwebs that spanned the length of the bunk.

At that moment, every emotion she had wanted to feel, every emotion buried so deeply inside of her, came pouring out. She fell on the ground and started crying like she had never cried before, sobbing and sobbing without being able to stop.

It was then and there that it hit her — the bird represented her people. They too had been trapped inside, desperately longing for freedom. They too had seen the sun and the world outside that tiny window, yet all they had been able to do was throw themselves against it in vain, only to fall back down into darkness.

She, Gila, was free. But really, she asked herself, how free was she? Free to go to parties and dances and shopping malls with her friends, free to wear the latest fashions and trade glossy magazines with her girlfriends, free to take long walks and do nothing but think about the meaning of life…

What kind of freedom was that?

Sitting there on the fetid filth-ridden floor of the

Auschwitz barracks, she realized for the first time in her life that, as a Jew, she had a responsibility to herself and to her soul. Being a Jew was something those six million had died for. It didn't matter if they were religious or not. Anyone with a drop of Jewish blood was taken, no matter how assimilated they were. They died for their Judaism! Now it was up to her — she had the chance to get out of this barracks and go back into the real world and *live* for it.

Slowly, she rose and dusted herself off. She wiped her face with a tissue and rubbed her eyes. Now she knew with absolute certainty that somehow, within this incomprehensible suffering, G-d was hidden. He was hidden, but He was there.

She stood at the doorway looking back down the length of the barracks at the tiny cracked glass in the window. No one else was there, and in a few minutes she would leave this place forever.

"*Shema Yisrael*," she whispered. Then she said it louder, and louder still, finally shouting at the top of her lungs, "*Shema Yisrael, Hashem Elokeinu, Hashem Echad!*"

She walked up and down the length of the barracks crying and shouting. And she knew that she would never look at life in quite the same way again.

Sure, she couldn't wait to get home to her family and her own room. But she now knew that as a Jew she had a responsibility and an obligation not to take her life for granted. She had to go and learn … because that was the only way she was ever going to be able to fly.

❧ *Every Step of the Way*

Many American Jews grew up in religious confusion. From parents, grandparents, and the broader community, they were exposed to a wide range of influences — from no observance, to Conservative, to modern Orthodox. In the search for sanity and peaceful relations, some homes adopted a policy of "live and let live." Often, parents would allow their children to make their own decisions when it came to religion. Sometimes a child, like the Rivki in this story, grew up in a home where she wasn't allowed to eat meat out of the house and no one drove the car on Friday nights, but at the same time everyone watched television on Shabbos. Understanding the conflicts of that misguided lifestyle, and the price paid by the generation caught up in it, can give us a better appreciation of those who were able to find the right direction, despite it all.

Rivki's first big decision came when she was 14. It was graduation time for the eighth grade. Her parents, in keeping with their "freedom of choice" policy, naturally left the choice between public school and Jewish high school up to her. Rivki saw herself as a normal all-American teenager, dedicated to having as much fun as possible. She didn't waste too much time deciding which school to go to, nor did her decision to attend a public high school come as a surprise to anyone. She and her mother went to register, and Rivki looked forward to starting the new year.

Then, a few weeks before school started, something happened that changed the course of her life. For some reason, she had trouble falling asleep one night. She tossed and turned in bed, feeling vaguely uneasy about something ...

It was about one o'clock in the morning. All of a sudden Rivki jumped out of bed and ran downstairs to her mother without even thinking. She found her mother standing in the laundry room, putting a load into the dryer.

"Ma!" she burst out crying, not even knowing what she was going to say, "I have to go to the yeshivah." She stood there with her mouth open, surprised at her own words.

"What did you say?" her mother asked. "That you decided to ... that you want to go to the yeshivah?"

"Oh my gosh, did I say that?" Rivki couldn't believe her ears. "I guess I did." She started crying again, from someplace deep inside her, a place beyond her conscious personality, a place of great importance.

The next day, her mother took her to the girls yeshivah. To her dismay, registration was already closed. Rivki stood there looking at the secretary and crying.

"Please, I just have to come here — I can't go to public school," she begged.

Finally the principal came out of his office to see who was making such a tumult. He invited Rivki and her mother into his office and, after an hour-long interview, told her that he would accept her "on the condition that she do well in her studies and maintain exemplary behavior."

She went to yeshivah — where she wasn't always happy. But she stuck to her end of the bargain. She received good grades and was very well behaved. In fact, she even got an award for excellence in human relations. Only much later, when she was already a seminary student in Israel, did Rivki hear the whole story. Her mother came for a visit, and their conversation turned to the fateful decision, and how she had come to change her mind. Rivki's mother then told her something she hadn't even remembered.

"You were 14 years old that night in the laundry room. Your father and I had been quite pleased with your decision to go to public school. But you looked at me with your face all red and puffy from crying and you said, 'Ma — I have to go to the yeshivah ... because there is more to life than having fun.'"

Dostoevsky Just Wasn't Enough

It is not often that we get a glimpse into the inner struggles that comprise life's direction-changing moments. Rebbetzin Freeman, a housemother at a well-known out-of-town girls seminary, shared this story with me about one of her outstanding students. How did she realize she was so outstanding? That's a story in itself. It was when they were cleaning together for Pesach that Rebbetzin Freeman noticed Irene's unique ability to organize and execute cleaning projects. She'd watch her and think, "I've been doing this for over 20 years and I never thought of that method!" Despite the work, she found herself drawing Irene into conversation. Since then, they've become friends.

"Irene's story can be a source of inspiration," she notes, "especially for those of us who have grown up with Torah and mitzvos and take so much for granted."

Irene was always searching. From the time she was old enough to read, she looked to language to define reality and experience. But Russian language books were devoid of anything to do with G–d. Although her scientist parents were atheists, they maintained a high standard that distinguished them from their peers. It wasn't only an intellectual excellence, either, but a certain morally elevated behavior that they demanded from Irene and her younger brother.

Irene's mother taught her how to read when she was five years old. Books became her way to reach out to the world beyond her ordinary Russian environment. She started devouring book after book, only later learning to discriminate. Yet even her favorites, all considered classics, couldn't satisfy her search for something more. How could she have known that she was seeking the religion of her ancestors, when even the slightest traces of Judaism had been wiped from Russian bookshelves? Books became her companions, and reading kept her mind wondering and her heart craving for something that would touch her soul.

When her family emigrated to the United States, to New York, her parents were faced with the problem of maintaining their standards of morality while providing the best educational opportunities for their teenage daughter. They chose an Orthodox school, fully confident that religious ideology would never "infiltrate" nor "spoil" their daughter's mind. Irene didn't want to go to a religious school, but as soon as she got to know her classmates and teachers, she fell in love with the place. She committed herself to treating these people with respect and dignity, even if she was an outsider.

Time passed and Irene started learning. Little by little, she accumulated information necessary for living a life that went beyond secular achievements. Strangely enough, she began to feel at home, and although she was not yet keeping any mitzvos, for the first time in her life her mind was not possessed of that terrible restlessness. She found herself believing in her Creator. A deep internal process had started and was gaining acceleration.

Then, during one school Shabbaton, a very unexpected and incredible thing happened. It was during the *Modim* (thanksgiving) prayer in the *Shemoneh Esrei*. Irene always used to feel very strange when she tried to pray, but she did so anyway. This time, as she was saying these words, it was as though a tiny spark in her heart that had lain dormant burst forth into flames and she knew, she just knew with her whole being, that Torah had to be at the center of her life. Within the next six weeks she became totally kosher and Sabbath observant. People told her to "go slowly." They said that it was risky to make such drastic changes so quickly. But she knew that although it seemed as if she were changing too fast, the process had actually been underway for years.

When they had lived in Russia, Irene's family, like most Russian-Jewish families, found it impossible to withstand the vehemently anti-religious restrictions of the time. Irene's great-grandmother was the last religious person in her family. When Irene started opening up to her classmates, she discovered that even in their families, somewhere along the line, someone had "left."

Now a student in a Jerusalem seminary, Irene is amazed that not even a few generations of "isms" were strong enough to put out the spark of Yiddishkeit in her soul. She is determined to do whatever it takes and make whatever sacrifices are necessary for her future. On more than one occasion Irene has said, "Intellectually, emotionally, and spiritually, there are no substitutes for Torah. Even the most brilliant minds in Western culture are groping around in the dark. I come from a family of scientists and strictly rational people. But an in-depth study of Torah reveals it to be a Divine masterpiece on life. I made my choice. My parents always taught me, 'Never aim for the mediocre. Investigate, examine, choose, and then shoot for the top.'"

Rebbetzin Freeman adds that a professor from a prestigious New England university once came to give a lecture to the girls on the Torah approach to science. Irene was an active participant in the question-and-answer period. Before he left, the professor told the housemother, "This girl is more brilliant than most of my graduate students!"

 The Real Operator

There's nothing unusual about a child feeling anxious about starting school for the first time, and little Motti Rabinowitz was no exception to the rule. Yet the surprise twist to the launching of his educational career is extraordinary. Divine Providence, with a little help from Motti's Yiddish-speaking Bubbie, Mama Rabinowitz, changed the course of his life.

Like the first-generation children of many immigrants to America, Mr. and Mrs. Rabinowitz were "traditional," but not quite as strictly Orthodox as their parents. That's why when the time came for them to send their five-year-old son, Motti, to school, they chose to register him in the local public school.

One morning in the later part of July, after he had gone with his mother to see his new school, Motti woke up feeling very scared. He thought about the big corridors, the dingy green walls, and the rows of chairs for all the children, most of whom he had never met. He got out of bed clutching his flannel security blanket and went to find his mother. She was sitting at the kitchen table. Motti climbed into her lap and buried his face in her neck.

"Mommy," he whimpered, "I don't like that school."

Mrs. Rabinowitz's heart sank. The first day of school was six weeks away and already her Motti was worrying? This was not like him at all. He usually loved new places and adventures.

Meanwhile, Mama Rabinowitz, who lived with her son and his family, had finished her morning prayers. Now, when she came into the kitchen to prepare breakfast, she took one look at Motti and immediately put a hand on his forehead.

"What's the matter, Helen?" she asked her daughter-in-law. "He doesn't have fever and he looks fine, so why isn't he dressed and outside playing already, as usual?"

Helen realized that her secret was about to be revealed and decided that it would be better for Mama to hear it from her than from Motti. Actually, she and her husband had decided to keep their decision to themselves until school started, but now ...

"Mama, Motti will be starting school this September," Helen said enthusiastically, giving Motti a bright smile. "Isn't that exciting? He'll learn the ABCs and how to read and write, and he'll make so many new friends. How wonderful — right, Motti, darling? So you see, Mama," she continued with an apologetic smile to Mama Rabinowitz, "he's a little nervous about going for the first time. But soon he'll be very excited about it!"

Mama wasn't fooled for one minute. Much to Helen's dismay, she had immediately sized up the situation. "Helen, *vos is dos*? He'll learn the ABCs?" her voice rose in a crescendo. "You're sending him to public school?!"

"Mama, it's the law in America, and, well, the truth is, we didn't really want him to go to such a religious school. He'll learn the *aleph-beis* from Zeidie, okay?"

Mama stood up and started pacing back and forth across the living room, a sign that she was very upset. Her brow was furrowed and her lips pursed. Zeidie was gone for the day, off to visit cousins in the country; she had stayed home, not enjoying travel in the summer heat.

She sat down in the frayed, gray armchair and took out her well-worn *Tehillim*. The hour hand made its way slowly around the face of the clock as she sat there saying *Tehillim*. Finally, she got up and went over to her daughter-in-law.

"Helen, Papa and I left Europe to save our lives. But without G-d, there is no life. If you send Motti to public school, who knows whom he might marry? You could, G-d forbid, have non-Jewish *kinderlach* for grandchildren!"

Mama started to pace back and forth again. Silence hung heavily in the room. She walked over to the living-room window which faced the main street. The outline of the brick apartment building across the street was softened by the tall leafy oak trees that lined the sidewalk. "*Ribbono shel Olam!*" Mama cried out. "Please — better I should die before I would ever see a non-Jewish grandchild from *mine* Motti!"

Bubbie went back to her pacing, back to the chair, and

back to her *Tehillim* for the rest of the afternoon.

When Motti's father came home from work that night, he had a long talk with his wife, after which he came into the living room to find his mother still maintaining her vigil in the gray armchair.

"Mama," he began. "I spoke with Helen. She told me how perturbed you are about Motti going to public school. We don't want you to be upset, so we decided to send him to a more traditional school. But it's up to you to make all the arrangements."

Actually, Motti's parents thought their idea was a clever one. This way, Mama would feel reassured that they weren't abandoning the family's Yiddishkeit. At the same time, with her broken English and only basic reading skills, she would probably be unable to make the arrangements necessary to enroll Motti in any school. By the time school began, her distress would have blown over, her efforts would have come to naught, and Motti's anxiety would have vanished.

That night, Mama couldn't sleep. All night she prayed, "*Ribbono shel Olam*, this is why you saved me from the gas chambers? To have *goyishe kinderlach*? *Mine* Motti has to go to a Yiddish school. He has to learn Torah." She remembered how her brothers used to sit with her father every day learning the *aleph-beis*. Now, 75 years later, the clear sweet melody rose up in her heart. Her eyes filled with tears as her indignation melted. "*Ribbono shel Olam*, I don't even try to understand You. Just please help me to put *mine* Motti in a Jewish school." Then she finally fell asleep.

The very next day, early in the morning, Mama Rabinowitz picked up the telephone and dialed directory assistance. After two rings, she received a prompt and courteous, "Good morning, may I help you?"

Mama took a deep breath and said, "I *vant* to find *de* Mine Street Yeshivah for young children, please."

"Pardon me, ma'am, the *what*?"

"*De* Yeshivah, *de* Yeshivah," Mama repeated.

The operator hesitated. Suddenly she remembered that two months ago a new listing had come in for a newly established school, Torah Yeshivah Academy. Why, those Rabbis who were running it spoke just like this woman! No question about it, that must be the place the lady was asking for.

"I have your number right here, Ma'am. It's a new listing. Please make note of it."

Mama dialed the number with cold, trembling fingers. A rabbi answered and Mama said, "Hello. *Gut* morning. I *vant* to register *mine* grandchild for school."

Was she surprised and relieved when the rabbi answered her in Yiddish!

Mama took Motti that very same morning and registered him for *cheder*. When she presented her son and daughter-in-law with the information that Motti was already registered in a Torah academy, they were speechless. After all, what could they say? It had been their idea to ask Mama to take care of it.

Little did they realize that the One who hears all prayers, sometimes directs His answers through an efficient telephone operator!

In Eretz Yisrael at the wedding of his oldest son, Motti stood up to speak. "Although my Bubbie is no longer with us, she must be acknowledged as the primary guiding force for our being here today. It was her vision and foresight at that time in

America that kept the Torah in our family. She knew that at the young age of five, I was already standing at a fork in the road. One path led to assimilation and intermarriage while the other led to vibrant Jewish lives. Bubbie took my hand and in her wisdom set me on the right path."

~ Bubbie Zisa

It was November of 1970. Rose sat on the bus, on her way to her weekly visit to her mother, who recently celebrated her 107th birthday. As she looked out the window, she marveled at how she was always moved to see the Land of Israel. It didn't matter that she had lived there over 25 years.

As the bus stopped at a red light, Rose allowed herself the rare luxury of a few minutes rest. She closed her eyes and thought back to times long past. She could still vividly picture the family house in the town of Hermanstadt, in the Rumanian part of Transylvania. She remembered the large outer courtyard, and the big backyard with two gardens, one for vegetables and one for flowers. Her mother's fondness for marigolds had produced a profusion of the colorful orange and yellow blossoming flowers, arranged in rows. The family didn't call them marigolds; they called them Bubbie Zisa's flowers.

Their home was filled with the happy sounds of a growing family of 10 children. Yet Bubbie Zisa had been childless for the first decade of her marriage. Heartbroken, she had gone with her husband to the Sanzer Rebbe for a *berachah*. His blessing that she would not only have children but *many* children, bore fruit, for not only did she raise her own brood, but years later, after she was widowed, she went to live with her daughter Gittel and her family, and helped raise *her* 10 children as well.

Although some members of the family spent devastating years in the camps, the entire family unbelievably survived the war, and they all came to Israel together in 1950.

Rose thought of her mother's piety. On the surface, she seemed like such a simple, unassuming lady, full of kindness for everyone with whom she came into contact. She was famous for the delicious *kichel* and the oversized *cholent* she made for Shabbos, and always received her children and grandchildren with a quiet ease and a ready ear. Her greatest joy was to see peace among her children. After dinner on Friday night in Hermanstadt, everyone would go to Bubbie Zisa for *zemiros*. Shabbos day they went straight from *shul* for *Kiddush* and *cholent*. The first night of Pesach everyone came to complete the second part of the *Seder* with her. And the second night they all gathered to count *sefiras ha'omer*. She drew people like a magnet, always remembering the names and birthdays of her 50 grandchildren, and numerous great-grandchildren.

But did anyone really know what lay behind her composure? Rose wondered. She herself knew a little bit. Often, over Yom Kippur her mother fasted "*a drier*," from the final *seudah*, through Yom Kippur, *motza'ei Yom Kippur*, and part of the next day.

"Mama," her children would beg her, "eat something!"

"Soon, *meine kinder*," she would say softly, stalling for time. Yet somehow, despite their protests, it wasn't until the next morning after her prolonged *Shacharis davening* that she finally would break her fast.

The immediate family knew that on Mondays and Thursdays Bubbie Zisa fasted. But most people knew her simply as the kind lady whose hands were always full of *lokshen kugel* and honey cake. Even at the age of 96, thought Rose with a surge of pride, Mama always went, laden with her care packages of *kugel*, traveling by herself, the length and breadth of *Eretz Yisrael* to visit her children, grandchildren, and great-grandchildren.

The green and white road signs told Rose that she would soon reach her destination. Good, sweet Mama, Rose sighed, nobody knows except me that the Satmar Rebbe of that generation stood up when you walked into the room. It had been Rose who accompanied her mother to the Rebbe following the death of her father. As soon as they walked in, the Rebbe stood up. Rose wished she could recall the conversation, but it was enough that she still had a clear recollection of the Rebbe's shining face.

The bus stopped at the familiar corner of her mother's street. Rose gathered her handbag, put on her jacket, and picked up a parcel of food she had cooked for her mother, as she did every week.

Rose knocked and then turned the key to her mother's tiny apartment. "Is that you, Mamma'le?" Bubbie Zisa called, as she raised her head from the pillow. "I'm very tired today, so you mustn't stay as long as usual. But there are a few things that I need to do."

Although everything was sparkling clean, Rose's mother asked her to change the bed linens and help her bathe. Rose had been there only an hour when her mother stroked her on her cheek, squeezed her hand, and said, "Go home, darling, I want to sleep now."

"Perhaps the doctor should come first and check you, Mama," Rose replied, with growing concern in her voice.

"No, it's not necessary. I feel fine. I just need to sleep. And you know I don't like you traveling at night."

Although it was unusual for her to leave so soon after she arrived, Rose kissed her mother good-bye and walked to the bus stop, resolving to call her sister and brother-in-law as soon as she arrived home and tell them to summon the doctor. No sense upsetting her mother and going against her request. After all, she seemed fine, just a bit more weary than usual.

As soon as Rose had left, Bubbie Zisa gathered up her strength and sat up in bed. She called her son-in-law and whispered, "Please come quickly."

Alarmed, he was by her side in no time. As soon as he saw his mother-in-law's face and her usual serene smile, he heaved a sigh of relief.

"*Zolstu zein gebentched,*" she greeted him warmly. "Thank you for everything. Please stand here. I want you to say *Vidui* with me." She then handed him her *siddur*, which they had recently bound once again because Bubbie Zisa refused to part with her old cherished volume. She had already opened it to the right place.

Her son-in-law took it with trembling hands. "But Mother, is this necessary? You look fine. Perhaps I should call the doctor?"

"No, *mein kinde*. Now hurry up, hurry up; the time has come."

She knew her time had come to leave this world. She was fully aware and fully conscious. Her son-in-law stood by her bedside and recited the *Vidui* with her in a choked voice. As soon as they finished, Bubbie Zisa closed her eyes and peacefully breathed her last breath.

Shaking, her son-in-law called the doctor, who came right away. Upon seeing his patient, he said tearfully, "I would gladly give 10 years of my life to have such a peaceful death right in my own bed. Her face is so tranquil. There is such a quiet radiance surrounding her, her *petirah* (death) could only have been the result of a Divine kiss."

❧ *Pesach Dream*

Selma Markowitz looks like a typical "down-to-earth" Bubbie. Now in her late 70s, her chesed activities barely allow her the time to visit her family in Yerushalayim. A grandmother of 10, she just celebrated the birth of her first great-grandson. In this story she shares a very special dream with us.

Mrs. Selma Markowitz awoke on Pesach morning with a heart full of gratitude. She had been saying *Tehillim* every day for more than 35 years but never before had she dreamt about *Tehillim*! She washed her hands and rubbed her eyes, then closed them again.

"It was such a beautiful dream," she mused. "I saw the whole network of stars cast in the blue-black sky like a silver fishnet. They were twinkling and gleaming. And I heard a voice saying, 'If you want freedom, say *Tehillim* 148.'"

In her mind's eye she returned to the *Seder* of the night before. Including the family, there had been 38 people. It was quite a colorful combination: The neighbors from Russia came with their children and grandchildren, there were five girls from seminary who hadn't flown home, and then there was Avraham Dickman, who had converted to Judaism a month before Pesach. Selma was wondering how her son, Lenny, was going to turn this hodge-podge of strangers into a cohesive *Seder* group, when, at the last minute, there was a knock at the door.

"Hello, is this the Markowitz family?"

"It is," replied her son. "Welcome, the answer is yes!"

In walked Roberta Furman with her backpack and travel guide.

"Are you the family who takes last-minute guests for the *Seder*?" she asked quietly.

"Yes," said Lenny, "the answer is yes."

Roberta had been traveling through Europe when on a last-minute whim she decided to fly to Israel for Pesach. She was a highly educated, earnest young woman from Wisconsin, who had never been to a *Seder*. She had gone to private schools, boarding schools, and was now on vacation from a prestigious northeastern university. It turned out that Roberta's questions kept everyone engaged in a lively conversation. The topic of freedom came up early at the table.

"Freedom," she said, in response to Lenny's declaration, "is the ability of an intelligent, reasoning human being to make choices and act on them for the betterment of humanity. But how can it have an absolute standard?"

"Ah," said Lenny, "then it's based on intelligence and on humanitarian concern for the world. But what about, G–d forbid, a murderer? Someone who does evil? He may think of himself as intelligent and good but he is really a threat to society."

Roberta pressed her eyebrows together. "Well, true freedom has to be for the good of the world," she answered.

"Yes," replied Lenny, "the Torah thinks so too. In fact, we define freedom as the ability to choose to serve G–d and do His will even when it is in conflict with our ability to behave 'freely' because G–d's will is for the good of the world."

The conversation went on and the *Seder* ended at a late hour. But this idea of freedom kept circulating in Selma's mind. She thought of her mother and grandmother who had escaped from the Nazis and lived in the basement of a gentile family's home for two years, barely seeing the light of day. Was that freedom? She thought of her friend's daughter who had run away from Yiddishkeit, started an export business in South America, and become extremely wealthy. Was that freedom?

Selma was usually so busy doing for other people that she barely had time to think about these concepts. Her "thoughts" were usually prayers for her children, grandchildren, and now this new great-grandson, that they should be healthy and strong and always on a true path in Yiddishkeit. As she cleaned the table, she murmured a prayer that everyone should recognize his or her purpose in the world to serve Hashem and that He bring all His lost children home.

As Selma dried the silverware, she remembered that two of her older grandchildren had come to her in the afternoon to ask her what Pesach was like when she was a little girl. "*Kinderlach*," she had replied gently, "I can tell you when we have time to relax and sit together. But right now, we have to finish up the work. I'm going to think about it so I can be ready to tell you all about it."

The liquid soap had a lemon scent, but as Selma's mind drifted back to the past, she could almost smell the fragrance of the sweet purple wine grapes as her father drove the family home from the produce market in his Model T Ford. Twelve weeks before Pesach, the preliminary aura of the holiday was felt in the house. Pesach belonged to her mother. She was the supervisor, and when it came to Pesach she was extremely disciplined. The first of the sacred tasks was making wine for the family and all the relatives. During the trip back from the market, it was Selma's job to watch the grapes. They were arranged in the back of the car, packed in oval-shaped baskets with heavy wire handles.

As soon as they arrived home, her father went down to the cellar and brought up the special oak wine barrel with the spigot on the bottom, and put it on a clean kitchen chair in back of the big black wood-burning stove. The wine-making marked the beginning of Pesach preparations.

As the time for the holiday drew closer, the excitement kept building until the kitchen and pantry were ready for the delivery. The icebox on the porch was stocked with ice by Tanta Chaika's husband, the iceman. Innumerable times during the final two weeks, her mother would repeat, "Don't touch it, your hands are *chametzdik!*" How Selma and her brothers and sisters managed to sneak away the jelly candies, she didn't remember. But somehow, everyone got a little bite.

Finally, *Seder* night arrived. Dressed in their best clothes, standing around the polished table with everything shining, Selma remembered that as a child, at the moment of *Kiddush,* she used to think that Hashem, Himself, was coming into their house. And now, here she was, in the Old City of Jerusalem with her eldest son and his family. "Dear G–d," she murmured, overwhelmed with emotion, "I'm so grateful."

It was three in the morning. Selma came out of the kitchen to check the table. All was clear and ready to be set for the day meal. She glanced towards the living room and saw Roberta in the black leather chair with her hand over her eyes. A muffled sob like the bleat of a newborn lamb escaped from her lips. Selma walked over quietly and stood by the chair. Roberta looked up and said, "I'm sorry I came. I mean, that didn't come out right. This is all so beautiful. I never knew such a thing existed. But my real life is a million miles away."

Selma wanted to put her arms around this Jewish daughter who had just had her first *Seder* at Lenny's table. But instead she patted her hand. "Roberta, my Bubbie gave me many treasures. I don't mean rubies or diamonds, I mean real treasures, words of wisdom. One of them I will share with you right now. Over and over Bubbie would tell me, 'My precious child, piety does not require great intellect, but a sincere heart.' I feel certain that if you are sincere in your search, G-d will help you to free yourself of whatever obstacles stand in your way."

Roberta looked up and touched the hand of the woman who had just spoken such nurturing words to her. "You know I would trade all my childhood memories for one *Seder* like this one in your son's home."

Selma's eyes filled with tears. "Roberta, G-d willing, one day you will make a *Seder* in your own home with your own *kinderlach*. It was Divine Providence that sent you here. Please get some sleep."

Selma had such a beautiful dream that night. "I had to pinch myself to believe it. I saw the blue sky filled with the brightest stars, twinkling so happily. And I heard a voice saying, 'If you want freedom, say *Tehillim* 148.' When I woke up in the morning I felt refreshed. I was so grateful to be alive, to be with my children in Jerusalem. After I said *Berachos* I went straight to my *Sefer Tehillim* to see what kind of a dream I had had. And there it was, the whole picture of Creation in that chapter of *Tehillim*, from the heavens to the earth, the whole idea of all the world existing for one purpose only — to recognize and praise Hashem. And who are we? A beloved people close to Him."

Our Sages (Berachos 57b) tell us that one who sees Tehillim in a dream can look forward to piety. Selma was truly a fulfillment of the words of her own Bubbie. It was through the sincerity of her heartfelt prayers and mitzvos that she merited, during Pesach, the festival of our freedom, to have such a special dream.

Torah Values

❧ Stubborn for G-d's Will

When we hear stories about great people, we are usually hearing about their triumphs, not their struggles. The triumphant success of Rebbetzin Devorah Sternbuch, who passed away at the age of 90, leaving 350 outstanding, G-d-fearing descendants, is impressive. But what is even more impressive is the story of how she overcame hurdles that would have defeated many a person.

Tragically widowed at age 35, Rebbetzin Sternbuch raised nine children, the oldest only 14, on her own. Instead of romanticizing her notability, let us instead realize that despite her illustrious ancestors, her personal greatness was born out of her responses to the difficult moments in her life. And consistently, without fail, these responses did not waver even a fraction of a millimeter from da'as Torah (Torah values).

The following composite of incidents were gleaned directly from a eulogy delivered by her son, HaRav Moshe Sternbuch. We are grateful to Rabbi Sternbuch for sharing his precious legacy with us.

A direct descendant of the Vilna Gaon, Rebbetzin Devorah Sternbuch grew up nurtured by the spiritual vitality of the *gedolim* (sages) of previous generations. It was part and parcel of the total atmosphere of her *chinuch* (education and upbringing). She was only 10 years old when she met Reb Chaim Brisker, but the meeting left such an impression on her that she would later tell her children about her memories of his face, his precision in pronouncing *berachos* (blessing), his cautiousness in avoiding problematic situations, his fervency in the performance of all mitzvos in a peerless manner, observing all particulars.

Halachah (Jewish law) was the guiding principle of Rebbetzin Sternbuch's life. Her son recalls: "London at that time was a spiritual desert. The whole outside world was against the type of life she led, replete with the most stringent Torah requirements. But she never gave in one iota. She could never be moved from her G-d, her religion. The Torah was also given in a desert, a wilderness, an allusion that one must observe the Torah wherever one is, in the desert, at sea, on land. A person must be prepared to walk through fire and water, if necessary."

In London, during the *shivah* (seven days of mourning) for her husband, with no one to turn to, she cried bitterly and frequently fainted. On the third day, the Rebbetzin's father came to comfort her. He also told her, "'*Sheloshah yamim l'bechi*, three days for weeping, and not more!' This is because G-d Himself doesn't want people to cry for more than three days."

She asked her father, "Is this a *halachah*?"

He answered, "Yes, it is."

From that moment on until her last day 55 years later, she was never seen crying over her husband's death! This seemingly superhuman adherence to *halachah* was the beacon for the preservation of Torah in her family, and it was this tenacious adherence to *da'as Torah* that saved their lives.

When World War II began, most Englishmen thought it would be of short duration. General consensus was that England and France would probably defeat the Germans in a matter of three or four months at the most.

The optimists, though, were soon sadly disappointed when they heard their prime minister tell the nation to prepare for a struggle that would probably last at least three to four years. Citizens were officially informed that, due to the recent events and a possible German blockade, all children would have to be deported by ship to the United States.

Many people did send their children out of the danger zone, and the Rebbetzin was desperate. She did not know what to do. Should she send her children to a secular, even non-Jewish environment? She wrote their grandfather asking him this question, and he answered: "Better that they die than risk becoming '*frei*' (irreligious) in America.

The Rebbetzin's worries grew by the day. The Germans began shelling London and air raids were frequent. Finally, she wrote to some distant relatives in the United States inquiring about the possibility of sending the children to them. The reply she received said she should send them, that America was not really as bad as all that, and that they would look after her children as if they were their own.

But Rebbetzin Sternbuch would not make a move without *da'as Torah* giving her a clear directive about what to do. She went to Rabbi Eliyahu Lopian asking that he cast the famous "*Goral HaGra*" for her.

Rabbi Lopian explained that this was not a simple matter but one which requires great concentration and even fasting on the day it is performed. He told her to return on Thursday the following week, when he would fast, and he promised to "cast the Gaon's lot" then.

She returned that Thursday but somehow, for reasons unremembered, Rabbi Lopian did not do the *goral* that day. He asked Rebbetzin Sternbuch to come back a week later.

In the meantime, she had booked passage for her children on a ship that took children from England to the United

States, in the event that the answer would so decree. The ship sailed that week, though, before she had an answer. That being the case, she kept her children in England, for she would never send them without having a *p'sak* (rabbinic decision) on the matter.

At the beginning of the following week they heard the shocking news that the ship on which she had booked passage had sunk, and that most of the children and adults on board had gone down with it.

The Sternbuch children had, thank G-d, survived due to their mother's stubborn insistence on acting only *after* she found out what the Torah had to say.

People who knew Rebbetzin Sternbuch used to say that with her around, you didn't need a *mussar* (ethics) book to learn from for she herself was a walking *mussar sefer*. When asked how she merited to have such illustrious offspring and descendants, all of whom are faithful to Torah-true Judaism, she would answer that she used to pray: "Please Hashem, You do what's Yours to do, and I'll do what I'm supposed to do."

"My mother's prayers were unique," says her son. "She used to pray loudly, always raising her voice to the point of crying out her prayers. In fact, she used to scream the *shul* down! The ladies complained to her saying they could not stand the way she shouted and raised her voice loudly like that. They threatened to complain to the Rabbi to have her removed from *shul*.

"She said she would join them, and they went together to the Rabbi of Adath Israel. The Rabbi smiled and said she should by all means stay where she was, for as long as her screams were heard from the ladies' section, the men had much better *kavanah* (concentration) downstairs, and in her merit their prayers were answered!"

In London, Rebbetzin Sternbuch ran a "*Hachnasas Kallah* Fund" for poor brides through which hundreds were helped. One day, a man who had already married off six of his children asked for help marrying off another. Somewhat embarrassed, he proudly stated that although he had already married off all his other children without having to ask for help, his financial situation was such that he had to come.

The Rebbetzin asked him to come back in a few days. One of her children, who had overheard the discussion, was surprised, and asked his mother why she had sent the man away. Rebbetzin Sternbuch paused. How much should she tell her child? This was an opportunity to teach her the proper approach to administering *tzedakah* funds, but she would be divulging someone's privacy. She said to him: "You see, I have already assisted him with the six previous marriages, and have also helped him with the seventh — without him knowing about it. But now that he has come here, I have to consult with a Rav about how to avoid embarrassing him."

Rebbetzin Sternbuch was famous for her strongly rooted *bitachon* (faith), and her *emunah* (firm belief) in the coming of the *Mashiach*.

"My mother," says her son, "always finished her conversations with 'may we live to witness *Mashiach*.' Her waiting for *Mashiach* was almost like a natural feeling. When I sat *shivah* I heard a story about my mother. The person said she had come to see my mother on *motza'ei Tishah B'Av*, to find out how she was feeling after the fast. Since my mother was advanced in age and hard of hearing, the lady had to pound on the door with all her might for quite some time before my mother opened it.

"When my mother opened the door, the woman saw a startled look on her face, as if she were expecting something to happen. Then my mother said: 'Have you got any news for me perhaps?'

"The woman said she'd just come to see how my mother felt after the *Tishah B'Av* fast. 'Oh,' my mother said somewhat disappointed, 'believe you me, I was convinced there must be some news about *Mashaich*'s coming when I heard you banging on the door like that!'"

Rebbetzin Sternbuch was a unique, extraordinary personality, who knew how to maximize opportunities for spiritual values.

"My mother always kept a lifeline link with *gedolei haTorah* (Torah sages)," her son relates. "I remember, for instance, Reb Elchonon Wasserman, who was very close to my father and to our family. My mother asked him for a blessing. Reb Elchonon blessed her that she should have children who were '*talmidei chachamim* (learned).' My mother thought it wasn't enough. She asked that the children should also be '*yirei shamayim* (G-d-fearing).' He promised that too, saying that was exactly what he had meant.

"Then she said, 'How about me? How will you bless me?'

"Reb Elchonon answered that when one has children who are *talmidei chachamim*, one is blessed with real *nachas* (inner joy).

"My mother said: 'I want you to bless me that the Almighty should have *nachas* from *me*!' And he blessed her again."

Rebbetzin Sternbuch used to say, "I'm coming to the *Yom HaDin* (Final Judgment). And *HaKadosh Baruch Hu* (G-d) will ask me: 'Nu, what's with you?'

"I will answer, 'I have raised a whole army in London, an army of Hashem!'"

The nachas she gave to Hashem in her life is now also part of her eternal reward.

A Mother's Sacrifice

When Avraham Avinu took his beloved son Yitzchak up to Har HaMoriah, they returned together. Our sages tell us that everything he did was with a heart full of pure joy. In this brief portrait of an event which took place nearly 200 years ago, we read of a mother's sacrifice for the spiritual welfare of her son. Miriam walked her 13-year-old son to the doors of the beis midrash (study hall) not knowing if she would ever see him again. Yet this young Lithuanian widow would not give in to her desire to have her only son with her in America. Avraham Avinu offered up his son once. Every single day for the next few years, Miriam built an altar and offered up her heart. It was the inner dimension of her suffering that was the foundation stone for her son's greatness.

The winter wind shook the shutters of the tiny house as Miriam prepared a breakfast of bread and hot milk for her son. In her mind, she once again reviewed the steps that had led to this fateful day.

When her husband passed away suddenly, she was left to raise their two teenage daughters and young son alone. Relatives in America invited her to immigrate, writing, "Don't be foolish. Make things easier for yourself and the children and come live with us." The choice to go or stay was a difficult one. She would need help to raise her children, yet she was reluctant to take her son from his yeshivah and risk jeopardizing his spiritual welfare.

After much deliberation, Miriam decided to send her daughters to their relatives in America while she would remain at home in Lithuania with David Yitzchak, their 13-year-old brother.

One day, after the girls had been in America for quite some time, the anxious mother received a letter from them:

> Dearest Mother,
>
> Shalom. We hope you are well. Life here in America is much easier than back home. Even though the work in the clothing shop is hard, it is so interesting to learn a new language and to meet new people.

When Miriam read the letter she felt her heart grow cold. There was nothing she could put her finger on, but intuition told her that her daughters' religious life was deteriorating and that they were in grave spiritual danger. She decided she had no choice but to make the trip to America and see for herself.

The trip would take at least a month. Travel by boat was

arduous, expensive and often dangerous. She would arrange for her son to be taken care of by friends and neighbors. Although the young David Yitzchak pleaded to be allowed to accompany her, his mother insisted his place was in yeshivah. There he would sleep, and eat his meals with neighboring families.

Yes, the decision had been a hard one, but now the day of her trip had arrived and there was no turning back. As Miriam set the cup of hot milk down on the table in front of her son, she studied his young face. It showed no signs of the pain he had already suffered in losing his father. Now he faced another challenge of equal magnitude.

As his devoted mother made sure his winter coat and scarf were fastened securely, she began to cry. "My precious child, you are dearer to me than my own life. I am going because I am afraid of what life is like in America for your sisters. I will send you letters as often as I can. Please, you must promise me one thing. You must keep your heart always in Torah. If you do, Hashem will bless you and bring you close to Him."

She walked David Yitzchak to the *beis midrash* and stood watching as he entered. The bitter wind whipped her with a bone-chilling cold but her heart was ablaze with prayer that was born from all her loss and suffering. "*Ribbono shel Olam*, I am doing this for You. I give You my child. Please take care of him and guard him day and night that his heart and mind will always be in Your Torah."

Miriam arrived in America shortly before Pesach. Her daughters were working in a clothing shop as apprentice seamstresses. When she saw their appearance her worst fears were confirmed.

"Don't worry, Mama. Life here is different but it's much better."

After a few weeks in America, Miriam faced a choice that broke her heart daily. If she left America to return to Europe, it would mean spiritual death for her daughters. If she stayed, she didn't know when she would see her precious son again. His letters caused her endless heartache.

> My dearest Mother,
> It is so hard here without you. I pray every day for your safe return. Mama, I'm so lonely. Please let me come to my family.

Upon reading this letter Miriam cried so much she actually fainted from grief. But nothing would break her resolve. She was determined to remain in America for the sake of her daughters and absolutely forbade her son to join them.

Years passed, and Miriam stayed in America to raise her two daughters as proper Jewish girls.

Her son was raised by the Father of all orphans and grew up to be the Rav of Dretchin.

Rav David Yitzchak was a respected figure not only amongst his fellow Jews but also amongst the neighboring gentiles. One night during World War I the commander of a platoon of Polish soldiers came to his house. The Rav received the Polish officer warmly, offering him some tea and schnapps.

"Rebbe," asked the commander, "give me a blessing that I and all my men will come home safely to our families."

The Rav looked at the soldier and said, "If you agree that you and your soldiers will never harm a Jew but will always treat them with kindness, then I will pray for you."

"Yes, Rebbe, I promise that for as long as I live, I will never harm anyone of your people and I will make sure my men obey that order."

The Dretchiner Rav blessed him, saying, "May G-d watch over you and your men that you return in health and safety."

And, in fact, the Polish commander and his entire troop returned home from the war unharmed.

In his later years, Reb David Yitzchak Magen, the Rav of Dretchin, came to Yerushalayim. Rav Aryeh Levin, *zt"l*, said of him that the giants of Yerushalayim were able to detect only some of his greatness. Reb Aryeh said that he was sure that Reb David Yitzchak merited being visited by Eliyahu HaNavi.

In these times of jet-age travel it is hard for us to imagine the extent of this mother's pain. When a loved one dies, G-d forbid, there is a special dispensation of comfort. But the continued separation by ocean and continent during a time when travel was expensive and difficult, and communication infrequent, kept this mother and son totally apart from each other. Nothing lessened the pain, yet in retrospect we can see that her choices bore fruit. May Hashem bless us that modern comfort and convenience do not become deterrents to the recognition of true values.

◈ No Stumbling Block

> *"There is abundant peace for the lovers of Your Torah, and there is no stumbling block for them" (Psalms 119:165).*
>
> *Reb Eliyahu Lopian comments that the title "lovers of Your Torah" applies particularly to women, who are not obligated to be students of Torah. It is the wife who demonstrates an unselfish love of Torah by enabling her husband and sons to devote themselves to Torah study.*
>
> *Men, on the other hand, are privileged to be students of Torah. At the same time, they are obligated not to waste time from Torah study. If they squander their opportunity to study, the Torah will become a stumbling block for them. Women, though, are very fortunate in that they enjoy abundant peace and security from their Torah activities, without fear of stumbling. They receive great reward for their love and support of Torah, but constant Torah study is not incumbent upon them, so they do not incur guilt for failing to study assiduously (Lev Eliyahu, vol. I, p. 286).*

Mrs. Luskavitz waved "good morning" to her neighbor Leiba and her young sons as they passed her cottage on their way to *cheder*. It was already the second week of school yet Leiba would walk the boys every morning instead of sending them off on their own.

"Perhaps," Mrs. Luskavitz mused, "the boys are shy. Poor

Leiba. It's not as if she has nothing else to do at home. Walking them there and picking them up every day is time-consuming. Well," she concluded, "they probably need a bit longer than most until they can get used to going by themselves."

But weeks passed and mornings found Leiba still walking the boys to *cheder*. Every morning, like clockwork, Leiba and her sons would wave to Mrs. Luskavitz as they walked past her house.

After two months of this, Mrs. Luskavitz could no longer contain her curiosity. Choosing a quiet moment in the middle of the morning, she knocked on her neighbor's door.

"Please come in," Leiba welcomed her with a smile. "What can I do for you, Mrs. Luskavitz?"

"Leiba, forgive me for asking. But for goodness sakes, it's been two whole months! The rains have started and winter will soon be upon us. I know your boys are sweet and shy but Leiba, for heaven's sake, send them in the wagon like everyone else. They'll get used to it!"

Leiba looked thoughtfully at her well-meaning neighbor. She hesitated for a moment as if trying to decide whether to share what was really in her heart. "Mrs. Luskavitz, I know you don't want me to overstrain myself. After all, we mothers certainly have enough work as it is! But permit me to share an experience I had when I was a teenager. You know, my father, of blessed memory, passed away when I was 14. We were a family of seven sisters and we all took care of our mother and each other as best we could.

"My uncle and aunt, newly married themselves, became like a second family to us. When their first son was three years old, he started *cheder*. It was a big *simchah* (joyous occasion) in the family. The day before, my aunt and uncle fasted and prayed. They gave *tzedakah* (charity) and invited relatives, friends, neighbors, and the poor of the town to a modest *seudah* (feast). I went with them to bring little Areh'le to his Rebbe for the first time. My uncle *bentched* (blessed) him, wrapped him up in his big *tallis*, and carried him to the *cheder* with tears streaming down his face.

"The Rebbe radiated goodwill and happiness. He was like a father to each of the little boys. He gave them the letters of the *aleph-beis* with drops of honey, dates, raisins and apples, so that their first taste of Torah would be sweet. It was very beautiful and touching.

"But, Mrs. Luskavitz," continued Leiba, "something else happened that day, something that made a lasting impression on me. On the way home, I saw a gentleman rushing through the street carrying what I thought was a little boy wrapped in a *tallis*. I assumed the boy was late for his first day of *cheder* and that his father was rushing to bring him there. Suddenly, a gust of wind lifted the edge of the *tallis* to reveal — a *Sefer Torah*!

"At that moment, I realized that every single Jewish child is like a living *Sefer Torah*.

"I took it upon my heart then and there that if Hashem blessed me with sons, I would do everything I could to dedicate them to learning Torah."

"But Leiba," said Mrs. Luskavitz, still puzzled, "how does that explain your taking the boys to *cheder* by foot day in and day out? Let them go learn Torah but send them in the wagon! They'll love it."

"You are right, Mrs. Luskavitz," Leiba replied softly, "children love to ride in the wagon. But I want my sons to learn," she said, her eyes misted with tears, "that they have to *work* to learn Torah. By working for Torah it will become their own and *b'ezras Hashem* they will be successful in their learning."

Before the war, in the little town of Grieva on the Russian-Polish border, a woman could be seen holding her two little sons by the hand, walking the long road early every morning and afternoon to cheder.

Both boys grew up to be Torah scholars of renown. One became a dayan, a Rosh Yeshivah, a Rav, and a posek, while his brother became a famous cheder rebbe, Reb Yitzchak.

Their mother Leiba's daily walk to the cheder and back again had resulted in the fulfillment of her vision. We can only imagine the heartfelt prayers that accompanied her footsteps, paving the way for her sons' success.

Forming the Cornerstones: A Tribute to Rebbetzin Rochel Fayge Wasserman z"l

> "... our daughters are like cornerstones crafted in palatial form" (Psalms 144:12).

Cornerstones are the stones at the corners of a building that unite the intersecting walls. They are the stones that the building rests on. They are the parts of an edifice, says Rabbi Shamshon Raphael Hirsch, that are not conspicuous, but recede into the background. Yet they are designed and built with consummate care and artistry.

> *So too is a Jewish daughter formed and molded to be the cornerstone that connects past and future. In this tribute to Rebbetzin Rochel Fayge Wasserman, z"l, Miri, who was one of her students over 50 years ago, gives us a glimpse of the meticulous and artful craftsmanship of a devoted teacher who knew she was shaping the cornerstones for future homes in Klal Yisrael.*

The building was rundown; the shabby classrooms occupied the upper floor. The old wooden desks had splintering edges, the blackboards were cracked, and the chairs wobbled on their slightly uneven legs. The rooms, hot and stuffy in the summer, were cold and drafty in the winter. No matter what the season, the air was always saturated with the pungent aroma of pickles and garlic sold in the grocery store below.

In that setting sat a teacher. Her appearance was the antithesis of all that surrounded her. The Rebbetzin came to class every day clad in a dress or a suit with a hat and shoes to match. The touch of jewelry, by no means ostentatious, just tasteful and modest, was a statement of her respect for her students and for her mission to teach Torah.

In the 1930s, American Jewry was racing headlong toward secularism and assimilation. When Miri's parents married during that era they made the highly unusual and unpopular choice to become observant. Together they made a decision to build a home based on adherence to Torah and mitzvos, and when their children were born they sought to give them what, in those days, in their locale, was defined as a maximum Jewish education.

It was only an afternoon school, two hours, four days a week, plus Sunday mornings. How much could a teacher accomplish in so little time? Especially having to combat the influence of the six hours of public school that preceded the lessons. But for Miri, those two hours when Rebbetzin Wasserman was her teacher were a brief interlude during which the foundation of her love of Torah and mitzvos was laid. Those two hours gave Miri the strength to carry home the new information about Torah life that brought about slow but lasting change and growth in her home. And the impact from those two hours four times a week are bearing fruit even today, a half century later, in third and fourth generations that are completely committed to Torah and mitzvos.

Rebbetzin Wasserman didn't seem to be daunted a bit by the fact that the class was made up primarily of girls who didn't come from strong religious backgrounds. She accepted each and every girl for who she was, loving her, caring about her, and letting her know that she was a worthwhile human being.

Rebbetzin Wasserman never just said, "Hello, how are you?" in a perfunctory manner, as many people do. She would ask, "How are you? How is your mother? How is your father? How are your sisters?" maintaining eye contact while waiting for an answer. She neither wanted nor expected a plain answer of *"Baruch Hashem,* everything is fine." A girl knew from her questions and the look in her eyes that the Rebbetzin very much wanted an honest answer. She was interested and she cared.

Her voice was always modulated with kindness, and her warmth and love expressed themselves in her acceptance of each student.

"She cared that each of us would succeed in her learning," remembers Miri. "For her it wasn't just coming and doing her job and saying what she had to say. She wanted us to learn. I remember how she would be personally hurt when someone behaved improperly. And so clearly I remember how she would check our written work. She held a red pencil in her hand as we stood next to her, watching. On her face was an expression of hope that she wouldn't have to use the red pencil. If I close my eyes I still see her hand moving across the lines as she read silently. If that hand with the red pencil didn't come to rest until the end of the page, she would whisper, '*Baruch Hashem.*' Then she would put down the red pencil, take up a blue pen, and with a smile write '*tov me'od*' (very good) on the bottom of the page. We were pleased — but she was overjoyed."

The Rebbetzin understood that her girls needed extra encouragement to continue their learning, so she gave recognition every step of the way. At the end of the very first *parashah* (Torah portion) they ever learned, they held a festive *siyum*. She didn't wait until the end of *Chumash Bereishis*, or until the girls had learned several *parshios*, she did it right away.

Although that *siyum* was held 52 years ago, Miri remembers it clearly today — in part, because it took place in her home.

"I even remember the cookies my mother and I baked for the occasion," she reminisces. "That's how much of an impression it made on me. But much more important, I remember the enormous feeling of pride and honor when both the Rav and the Rebbetzin came to our house that day.

"Imagine two people of such stature coming to a *siyum* made by less than a dozen young girls, aged about nine or ten. How proud we were! What a special occasion it was for all of us. That was Rav Wasserman and the Rebbetzin. Everyone was important to them. Nothing was too small if it had to do with loving people and bringing them closer to Torah."

On the bookshelf today in Miri's home rests a small *siddur* that was given to her as a prize when she was in the fifth grade. The inscription was written by the Rebbetzin those many years ago in impeccable Hebrew, with every vowel carefully in place. At the time Miri received it, the Hebrew was totally unintelligible to her. It was only about 20 years later, when she came on *aliyah* and Hebrew became her second language and an integral part of her life, that she finally understood every word.

At the time that she wrote the words, the Rebbetzin knew that reading them was beyond her student's ability. She never said a word but Miri now knows that the message was clear.

The inscription reads: "I am not worried. You will continue to learn. And one day you'll understand what I've written here."

Baruch Hashem, she was right.

Miri was the Rebbetzin's student for many years. Even after the Wassermans moved to another city, Miri and the Rebbetzin remained close through correspondence. When Miri married, the Rebbetzin was unable to attend the wedding because she did not want to leave her students without a suitable substitute and none was available. Missing that special day was a sacrifice, but part of her way of life.

The Rebbetzin wrote Miri a letter, explaining why she was not coming to the wedding. In response, Miri wrote a letter back, telling the Rebbetzin what it meant for her to have had such a wonderful teacher over the years.

The Rebbetzin answered that letter. Perhaps nothing could give us a better glimpse into the greatness of her character than these words she herself wrote to Miri a few weeks before the wedding.

"Your statement that I was an inspiration to you in your

Torah studies gave me tremendous joy — although I don't feel in me the power and the sufficient Torah knowledge to be able to instill in my students that high and great esteem and deep-rooted understanding for the holy and great moral values of our Torah as you seem to have. You surely had much greater and much more learned teachers from whom you absorbed this love and understanding of our great Torah inheritance. But if in any way I also was an influence and inspiration to you, I am surely extremely happy.

"I will tell you that if not for my teaching that I so wholeheartedly undertook, I would not be able to go on in my private life. All my interest and aim was the children, that the children should not leave the class without gaining and learning from every lesson. I used to be heartbroken when I felt the class didn't accomplish more or didn't absorb the lesson. I took my teaching very sincerely. Maybe this is what left an influence on my pupils. Anyway, it brought tears to my eyes when I read your letter. I really feel I'm overestimated and that I may yet learn a lot myself. And surely, I am not as great as you think I am. I don't want you to be misled into thinking that this is a great woman. I surely can't compare to a great one. Maybe due to our poor generation I also am considered to be something."

Yes, Rebbetzin Wasserman, it may be a poor generation but you made it much, much richer because you were part of it.

❧ The Garment Factory

In stark and striking contrast to the sweatshops of yesteryear, this portrait of a Jewish factory illustrates how the practical humanity of Torah values extends to everyone, Jew and non-Jew alike. A position at the Ideal Shoulder Pad Company was fiercely sought after. And who was the inspiration behind it all? Credit must be given to Bubbie Annie, because truthfully, the factory was her brainchild.

Bubbie Annie was concerned with much more than the financial survival of her family. Her motivation in starting the factory was to give the family an independent economic base so that they could all remain Torah-observant Jews. The times were rough, and the battle to make a living in a six-day workweek (with Sunday the one day off) had many casualties.

The story of Bubbie Annie was told to me by a dear friend and neighbor, Rabbi Asher Margoliot, z"l, whose sudden passing left those of us who knew him in tremendous shock. I had the privilege of hearing this piece of unknown contemporary Jewish history directly from Reb Asher. Since he was such an erudite and eloquent speaker, this fascinating portrait has been left in his own words. May it serve as a small contribution to the memory of both R' Asher and his wife, Channa, z"l, and an inspiration to us all.

"My grandmother, whom we called Bubbie, was named Annie Rosenthal. Annie Rosenthal was a well-known figure to the leaders of the Jewish community of East New York, Brooklyn in the early 1900s. Rabbanim from the big *shuls* would come to discuss matters of Yiddishkeit with her, as well as political issues, all of which benefited from her common sense approach. They would come and explain the problematic situation over a glass of tea and say, 'Mrs. Rosenthal, what would *you* do?'

"In later years, after I grew up and left home, I would meet people, pillars of the community, who had known my grandmother, and they would say, 'You are Mrs. Rosenthal's grandson! Do you know who she was?'

"The two most outstanding areas for which I think my Bubbie should be remembered are in what she did to insure that both her family and the members of the community would remain Jewish, and that the children who were growing up in Brooklyn in the beginning of the 1900s would be able to lead Torah lives. At this time in Brooklyn there were really no *yeshivos gedolos*. Chaim Berlin and Torah Vodaath were just starting, but even these institutions had only elementary schools or *kollels*, nothing for the high-school age. So there was a problem not only for her own children, but for all the children in the community.

"Bubbie's first step was to convince my Zeidie, R' Avraham Rosenthal, to open a family business. She argued that the children would not be able to make a living in America and still remain Torah- and mitzvah-observant Jews because, at that time, everyone had to work on Shabbos. She said the only solution — and not only for the needed income but also in order to give them meaningful work — would be to work together in a family business. They shopped around and decided to open a factory which they named the Ideal Shoulder Pad Company, Inc. This was the first *shomer Shabbos* factory in the New York women's garment industry. They made shoulder pads, which had come back into fashion, and something called a 'sleeve head,' a little piece of material that extended down from the shoulder pad to give more body to the top of the sleeve.

"When they started the business, they moved to an apartment in the city, just opposite the first factory, because my Bubbie still had nursing children. She always had a baby in a basket or bassinet near her sewing machine. When she worked on the sewing machine in the factory loft, she could see their house right across the street. Whenever a baby who was still at home needed to be nursed, one of the older girls would pull down the window shade. That was the signal for Bubbie to go home and nurse the baby.

"The children were basically brought up in the factory, in the sewing shop. Eventually, the family moved back to the East New York section of Brooklyn to live, but kept the factory in Lower Manhattan. You'll be surprised to hear that the factory is still in existence today, on a very, very small scale. Nowadays, there are prestigious law firms, accounting firms, and other prominent businesses in Manhattan that have *minyanim* and offer *shiurim*. In Bubbie's era, though, this factory was one of the first ones to do so, at least in the women's garment industry in New York. Non-Jews loved to work there because they would get off not only on all American federal, national, state, and legal holidays, but they would also get off on the Jewish holidays as well.

"Workers began their day at 8:30 a.m. instead of the current 9:00, and they had only a half-hour lunch break as opposed to an hour because, on Fridays, they would work only half a day. Bubbie and Zeide closed the factory on Fridays at the same time both winter and summer, because, as my Zeidie used to say, 'How can I begin to explain to all my workers that in the winter we work these kinds of hours and in the summer we work these kinds of hours?

Anyway, in the summer we often go away for Shabbos and we're going to need time to travel so we will close on *erev Shabbos* at 12 o'clock all year round.'

"Everyone in the family (all nine of us) was involved in the business. The girls all worked on the sewing machines and padded the shoulder pads, and the men cut them, boxed them, delivered them, and took care of making the sleeve heads. I remember many a time as a child, when I was on vacation from elementary school, going up to the loft in the factory and falling asleep in the bales of muslin they used to stuff the shoulder pads.

"Once a year they used to have a picnic for all the workers. My Bubbie would say, 'We have to show the workers that *Yidden* appreciate the work they do. We wait for a nice summer day and take everyone for a picnic, where we can get involved in playing sports, separate for men and women. They'll see that we wash before eating, they'll see that we *bentch* afterwards, and we can show them a good time at the expense of the business.'

"This year when I went to America, I tried to reach a cousin, the only cousin still in the business. Everyone else sold out their shares either right after they got married or somewhere along the line. The business is now very small, located in Long Island City and, although I was able to reach my aunt and uncle and speak with them, I wasn't able to reach my cousin. I had no phone number to leave where he could catch me, since I was traveling all over the country.

"In desperation, on my last *erev Shabbos* in America — and I had a flight out that Sunday — I tried calling him at work. A factory employee answered the phone. When I asked for my cousin, he told me that he was not in. 'Please help me,' I said. 'I am a cousin visiting from Jerusalem. I'm leaving on Sunday, and I really want to speak to him.'

"The employee, who was obviously not Jewish, replied, 'If you're from Jerusalem, then I don't have to tell you what Shabbos is. Your cousin is going to be at his parents' house for Shabbos. Now, I don't know what time Shabbos is in Jerusalem, but you should know that here, you can't call after 4:30. So please give him a call at his parents' home. He'll be there and you'll be able to reach him.'

"I almost cried as I hung up the phone, because I realized that my Bubbie and Zeidie's dream is still alive. They have been gone for many years; their children, almost all of them, are not alive and certainly not around to work in the business. However, the dream of having a *shomer Shabbos* factory where even the non-Jewish employees can tell you when Shabbos is or what Shabbos is, is still very much alive.

"And even though I myself have been to many factories and businesses where a switchboard operator will announce on the loudspeaker, 'Time for *Minchah*,' and I have seen companies which have set aside hours for Torah study in their board room, all this is part of the 1980s and 90s. In the early 1900s, this was a dream — the dream which kept everybody in the family *shomrei Shabbos* while being able to earn a living."

✒ *A Sister's Wisdom*

At the time of this story, Mindy Shapiro was only 14, the second child in a family of eight. She already showed signs of the compassion and caring that later developed into a tremendous ability to teach special children. Today she runs a school for the physically handicapped and trains teachers who are about to enter this demanding field.

𝓑eth Shapiro stood in the jewelry store imagining she was standing inside the middle of a crystal prism. The whole world was glimmering with rainbow, incandescent reflections. She stood with her seven-year-old nose pressed against the clear glass display case. She had never seen such jewels before! The world of opal, amethyst, diamond, carnelian, pearl and coral stood before her. She looked down at the bubble-gum-prize ring on her finger and knew it would never again seem quite so precious.

Beth had gone shopping with her elderly aunt, who was a widow with no children of her own. It was their way of spending the afternoon together. Although Tante Tzippi had heart trouble and had to carry nitroglycerin pills in her bag, she had never lost a certain youthful vivaciousness. Out of the blue, every now and then she would tell Beth, "Today is a fun day. Let's go out for ice cream!" And despite protests and warnings about cholesterol from her worried sister, Beth's mother, Tante Tzippi would take her by the hand and they were off into a world of their own. They went to a place where cardiologists were not allowed to enter and where the heart of a little girl was made to feel special.

That day, after the chocolate ice cream, Tante had announced, "I need to have my gold earrings fixed. Let's go across town to the jeweler." She took Beth on a bus for the very first time and they got off under the Lexington Avenue uptown railroad tracks to go to the jewelry store. As the jeweler explained what needed to be done to her earrings,

Beth heard Tante Tzippi ask, "Do you have anything especially for children?" He brought out a tray of rings.

Beth felt a warm hand on her shoulder breaking her trance-like stare at the jewelry case. "Look, darling, do you see something you like? Tante wants to buy you a present." Beth looked up at her in wide-eyed disbelief.

"Mama won't let me, Tante Tzippi," she whispered.

"It's a present, darling, it's okay."

Beth's hand was cold as she picked out a tiny amethyst heart centered on a gold ring. It fit her ring finger perfectly. Tante Tzippi gave her a kiss and said, "A special girl like you deserves to have a special present from her Tante." Beth was very happy and felt very grown up. She put her bubble-gum ring in her pocket and thought of her three-year-old cousin Mashie who would want it.

When they arrived home, the ring was met with cries of "Oh, Tzippi, how could you get her something so expensive!" But Tante, with her typical fun-loving, spunky side, replied, "It gives me more pleasure to spend it on her now than after I'm dead! Besides, when I'm dead you'll use the money for practical things and she'll never have anything pretty."

That night it was Beth's turn to clean out their parakeet's cage. She put newspapers on the floor, and of course took off her precious new ring because she didn't want to get it dirty. After she finished with the cage, she quickly rolled up the newspapers and took them to the incinerator chute.

When she went back inside the apartment, she looked all over for the ring. She couldn't find it anywhere. She felt a cold emptiness in her heart and her stomach knotted up. Her ring, her beautiful new ring was lost forever in the incinerator chute!

One glance at the stern look on her mother's face and she burst out crying and ran to the bedroom she shared with her two older sisters.

Within two minutes Beth's sister Mindy came and quietly sat down next to her on her bed where she lay sobbing, her face buried in the pillow.

"Beth," she began gently, "one day, *b'ezras Hashem*, I will buy you another ring. I can't do it now, but when I get older and have more money, I will buy you a beautiful ring, as pretty as the one from Tante Tzippi. But right now I want you to try to understand something: In our house, we don't cry about *things*. *Baruch Hashem*, we have a wonderful family and there are so many people who love you. And we have Torah.

"Look, honey," she said, reaching for a *Sefer Tehillim*, "you are learning to read so well. What does this say?"

Beth had planned to stay buried in her pillow because she was too embarrassed to show her red, puffy face. But her sister's appeal to her new love and passion, reading, aroused an unbearable curiosity. She picked up her face from the wet pillow and looked into the *Sefer Tehillim*. Slowly she read in a whisper, "*Tov li Toras picha mei'alfei zahav vachesef* — The Torah from Your mouth is better for me than thousands in gold and silver."

Her sister looked deep into her eyes. "Even if you had a thousand rings like that, our Torah is much more precious. Tante Tzippi loves you very much and she wanted to buy you a special present. Don't worry, I'll help you tell her the ring was lost. She might be upset, but you'll apologize and she'll get over it. But in our house, sweetheart, we never cry about things like rings."

Her sister looked down at her with a smile and brushed her tear-damp hair away from her eyes. "Rings are things and things are fine, but they won't give you happiness. We have something better than gold: Torah!"

Beth hugged her sister in a wordless thank-you. Little did she know how profound and lasting an effect those words would have on her throughout her lifetime.

✥ Divine Pipeline

Mrs. Silverman was always looking for ways to educate her children about how to appreciate the Hand of Hashem in their lives. This story is a perfect example of how self-restraint in mothering turned into a teaching of Divine rescue.

In their house near the Eastern Pennsylvania train tracks, where the walls shook when the trains rattled past, the Silvermans were too poor to have a refrigerator. They used an icebox. Every day, Mrs. Silverman would buy a piece of ice from the neighborhood iceman for 15 cents. She would put it at the top of the box. There was nothing to keep the ice frozen, so as the day went on, the ice would melt and drip down into the special water pan that caught the drops. People who could afford it would hire a plumber who connected a pipe so the water drained through the wall to the outside of the house. But in the Silvermans house, they had a pan.

Children's play 70 years ago was much different from what it is now. They didn't have blocks and they never heard of Lego. They had empty matchboxes, burned-out matches, cardboard boxes, wooden crates, scraps of fabric, and twigs and pebbles from the backyard — yet they never felt deprived.

And for real fun, what better game than to chase a younger sister all over the house threatening to drench her with all the water from the icebox water pan?

For nine-year-old Moshe, that was the highlight of his day. The funny thing was, his mother never really stopped him. All she would say as little Raizel hid in the folds of her skirt was, " Moshe, now that you are holding it in your hands, would you please empty the pan before you put it back."

And that's how Moshe was promoted to the distinguished position of chief icebox-pan-emptier ... until that fateful day when he forgot.

To understand what happened that historic Yom Kippur, it is important to know that in their living room, which was also the dining room, they had a large round oak table which stood on a pedestal, with three thick lions' claws encircling the base. And to get the full picture you also have to know that the only event for Moshe that was more exciting than dumping the water pan down an unsuspecting sister's back, was having live chickens in the house on *erev Yom Kippur*. Then he was kept busy the entire morning scaring poor Raizel with the chickens. He would chase after the rooster, causing it to fly around the living room in a panic, while Raizel stood there crying and laughing at the same time.

One particular *erev Yom Kippur*, Moshe was very busy chasing the chickens around the living room, too busy to empty the water pan.

After Moshe's mother *bentched licht* that day, the whole family went to *shul*. The candles were left flickering in the middle of the lions' claws table. Suddenly, they toppled, and the tablecloth burst into flames! The fire burned a large hole in the material, which, blazing like a torch, fell to the floor.

At the very same time, the water pan overflowed. It covered the floor with water and extinguished the fire.

The family came home and saw the miracle. Mrs. Silverman seized the opportunity and said, " Moshe, you were so busy with the rooster today, it was meant to be that you should forget about the water pan."

"Little Moshe," who is now well into his 70s, still relishes telling about his mother's wisdom. "She didn't scold me for forgetting. Really, it was so clearly the Hand of Hashem." And the water pan, instead of being a sign of poverty for the Silvermans, became a symbol of their personal connection with their Creator. So much so, that there family credo was, "Don't worry — just remember the pan."

Thursday's Test

Esther Wycoff is the mother of a large family. Her husband learns in kollel. When her youngest child turned five, Esther, a former kindergarten teacher, went back to school to study computers and technical writing, professions that can easily be pursued at home. Before relating this story she confided, "I did not grow up frum. This lifestyle is totally different from anything I ever imagined for myself. There are times when I just can't trust the natural responses of my personality because they stem from secular values. Every choice I'm faced with must always be held up to the light of Torah and eternity, otherwise I would wind up paying lip service to priorities but handing over values that are not really whole.

"Sometimes," she continued, "when I read about very great people, even though I enjoy hearing about their lives and I do get inspired, I also feel almost forlorn. What could I possibly do in my own life that could even begin to compare to how they lived?

"But when I really think about it, of all the possibilities available, the healthiest, most rational choice is to live a Torah life. Torah has to come first. But — that's a very lofty aspiration. In the daily routine of life with all its myriad details, it's not always easy to put that value into practice!

"Take, for instance, what happened to me last Thursday," she said.

When Esther went back to school she knew her schedule was going to be extremely demanding. Yet she was determined to keep her household running smoothly. Since Thursday morning was her only time off, she set it aside for completing all her Shabbos preparations. Even the children had weekly tasks so that by nighttime everything could be ready — even the table was set for *Kiddush*.

Six months passed and Esther was excited about the progress she was making. It would be wonderful to be able to work at home and enable her husband to continue learning.

One Wednesday night, just before she fell asleep, she replayed a conversation she had had that day with a close friend who was coping with a chronic illness. "Esti," her friend had said, "we don't realize how grateful we should be for an ordinary day."

As her friend's words echoed in her mind, Esti's heart filled with gratitude for all the blessings in her life. The midnight quiet gave rise to inspiration, and instead of sleeping, Esti reached for her journal and her pen.

"Dear G-d," she wrote, "please bless us with the joy of an ordinary life. Let me appreciate the motions of an 'uneventful' day with such 'boring repetitions' as washing dishes and seeing them sparkle. Let me appreciate how You in Your utmost kindness make the sun rise daily and take us through the seasons and cycles of the year. Let me be aware of how Your moon stands for renewal each month and then hides itself in the darkness of concealment, and how Your stars pulsate like clockwork in the night. Let me move in Your world with a pattern as deliberate as the sun, moon and stars, yet always above their orbit. Let me be 'as usual' against the backdrop of the night, as the darkest moments pass and we inch through history towards the dawn."

The next morning, Thursday, Esti sat in the kitchen having coffee with Bluma, a school friend and regular Wednesday overnight guest. All the children had left for school, or so she thought, and in another few minutes she would drive her husband to *kollel* before beginning her day. Suddenly, she spotted an enormous puddle right in the middle of the living room.

"How strange," she murmured, standing up to take a better look. "Bluma! Take a look at this — the living room is filling up with water!"

A closer look afforded no clue as to where the water was coming from. Esti tried to squelch her rising panic. She had a computer exam on Sunday; her writing sample was due two days later. Where was this water coming from and how much of her precious time would it take to fix it? Worse, how would she cook for Shabbos if the water had to be turned off?

Bluma's voice cut into her racing thoughts. "Look over here, Esti. It looks like a bubbling fountain." Her friend's normally appreciated poetic way of speaking did nothing to calm Esti. She looked over to where Bluma was standing. Sure enough, there it was. Had she been in the woods or at the edge of a bubbling brook on a Sunday afternoon, the sound would have evoked feelings of peace and serenity. But this "natural spring" freely flowing up through her living-room floor tiles created no such feelings!

At that moment, Esti's five-year-old son, Moshe, walked in. "*Ima*, the bus to *cheder* didn't come. Now I can't go, 'cause I don't wanna be late," he whined.

"Hey! What's this, *Ima*? Yippee, water!" he cried, as he started splashing in the water and dancing around the middle of the living room.

Okay Esti, she said to herself, *think fast. Plan A: Take the easy way out, let Moshe stay home today, ask husband to handle the water while I go out to shop and study. Plan B: Drive Moshe to cheder, drive husband to kollel, call the landlord, buy ready-made Shabbos food, pray for help with studying.*

"*Ima*, why don't you turn off the water!" Moshe called, still enjoying the by-now mini-lake in the living room.

Smart kid, she thought. *Why didn't I do that ten minutes ago?*

"Sorry about breakfast, Bluma," Esti called over her shoulder as she ran to the back porch. After turning off the water main (and changing Moshe's wet socks) she made her decision.

"Okay, today *Ima* is the bus driver," she declared in a voice that left no room for argument. "Let's go." Then she called their landlord about the leak. He told her not to worry about it, that he had insurance, and said they should wait for a call from his plumber, who only worked afternoons.

Somewhat relieved, Esti gave him their cellular phone number. "Bye, Bluma," she called out from the front door as she and her husband left the apartment with Moshe in tow.

As they were pulling out of their parking spot downstairs, Esti's husband noticed a little blue truck in front of the building. On the side was painted in big white letters, "Pepperford's Plumbing Company — 150 years of good service."

"Wouldn't it be amazing," he commented, "if that was our landlord's plumber?"

"Sure would," his wife replied, "but he said not until the afternoon, so let's just hope it gets fixed before Shabbos."

They delivered Moshe to his Rebbe with a minimum of protests. Inside, Esti was churning. She fought hard to clamp down on her urge to ask her husband to stay home and help. She felt she had plenty of good reasons to ask him to handle both the plumber and any extra work the problem would cause.

But underneath it all, she tapped into a deeper strength. *Let him go learn*, she said to herself. *Somehow, things will work out.*

Upon reaching the *kollel*, they said their good-byes and Esti went home to face the water music herself.

No more than half an hour had passed when the phone rang. Bluma answered it. Her face revealed all the surprise she felt at hearing whatever the voice on the other end of the line said.

"Okay, I'll tell her," she said, and hung up. "Esti, you're not going to believe this. It was the plumber and he said he'll be here in ten minutes. He's been in the building since

7:30 this morning — right next door! All he has to do is transfer his tools and get to work."

Esti was speechless. She ran to the living room to move the desk so the plumber could get started right away. He arrived within minutes.

"See this?" he announced triumphantly as he pulled a piece of rusty pipe out of the hole he chopped open in the floor. "Here's where the water was coming from. It's got a hole in it.

"Funny thing is, I just fixed exactly the same problem in exactly the same place in your neighbor's living room! So don't you worry, in less than an hour, you'll have your water back on."

"This has got to be one for the books, Bluma," Esti said. "Hashem knew we would need a plumber so He sent him even before the leak!"

By midday, the only hint of the morning's disaster was the gaping hole in the living-room floor. Other than that, order had been restored, the washing machine was purring, and the kitchen had its usual Thursday afternoon cornucopia of fruits and vegetables arrayed on the counter waiting to be washed.

As her husband walked in for lunch, with the joy of having spent his morning immersed in learning apparent on his face, Esti felt elated. She knew he was expecting a mess and she couldn't wait to see his reaction.

He was amazed.

She smiled and said ebulliently, "A *tzaddik* decrees and Hashem fulfills!"

He said, "Esti, what are you talking about?"

"Remember that blue plumbing truck we saw on our way out this morning? Well, you were right! It *was* our landlord's plumber. He'd been in the building since 7:30 this morning. And do you know where? Right next door!"

Esti did better on her computer test than she did on the writing sample, but she knew in her heart that her real test had been to show Hashem how much Torah meant to her. And she had passed it with flying colors! Pipes could burst, floors could be flooded, but set times for learning Torah were not to be disturbed.

It's easy to think, "What's the big deal? What's the big mesirus nefesh?"

But if we take a deeper look into Esti's circumstances, we might come to a different conclusion. Esti grew up in a small town in Pennsylvania, received a public-school education and, aside from Yom Kippur, when her father sat in the family room of their ranch home reading the Daily Gazette and fasting until three stars came out, she barely knew she was Jewish.

After finishing college, she took the summer off to travel and "somehow" landed in Israel. There she found her way to Jerusalem, where she stayed for two years studying in a womens seminary.

At the time of this story, Esti had eight children and her husband was learning full time. With no internal points of reference from her own upbringing to rely on, with no extended family network to lend a hand, and with the emotional isolation and loneliness that are the consequences of her choice to become religious, Esti knows that the fate of her family's spirituality rests with her. The Thursday the pipe burst was an ordinary day with ordinary challenges. But Esti's finding the inner strength to send her husband to kollel was, for her, an act of extraordinary self-discipline and faith.

After 120 years, one of the questions men are asked is, "Did you set aside fixed daily times for learning?"

But what about women? Maybe one of the questions we will be asked will be, "Did you let your husband go to learn at his set times?"

❦ Park Bench Realization

Four o'clock one summer afternoon found Bayla and Miriam, close friends as well as neighbors, sitting on a park bench enjoying the fresh air. Their youngest children dug in the sandbox, while their older boys sped down the bicycle path. It had been a good day, measured in the small but meaningful markers of the average young mother's day: The school buses had been on time, every child's clothing had been laid out the night before, and a defrosted casserole satisfied everyone for lunch. It was Bayla's hope that the rest of the day would go just as smoothly.

Suddenly, an unexpected comment made by her friend jolted Bayla into a new level of appreciation for all those prosaic chores that so filled the days of her life.

Isn't that what friends are for?

Miriam was the class dreamer, bright and full of deep thoughts about everything. It was hard not to get impatient with her when shopping, because she agonized over every purchase. Once she read a book about color therapy and for three weeks after that her friend Bayla refused to go shopping with her. Soon enough, though, they were back to their usual companionship. When you've been friends since nursery school, it's impossible to stay apart.

"Bayla," said Miriam, turning to face her friend, "I know you don't like to philosophize and you think I'm too deep, but I have just got to tell you this because it made me so happy and I think it'll do the same for too. Okay?"

Uh-oh, thought Bayla. She had no idea what Miriam had in mind this time, but for the sake of the friendship she was willing to suffer through 10 minutes of philosophy. Hopefully, that's all it would be.

"What is it?" she asked, mustering up a decent amount of curiosity. Truthfully, she was grateful to have a friend who brought more depth and meaning to her life.

Happy to have the go-ahead, Miriam launched into her thought-for-the-day. "My husband told me this last night and I can't stop thinking about it. Do you know that the *cheder* learning of Jewish children is more precious to Hashem than the rebuilding of the *Beis HaMikdash*? He explained it to me with some of the Maharal's commentary. He said that Torah is beyond this world, and that Jewish children are so pure and free of sin that the Torah they learn is totally pure and holy."

Now this was a thought that struck a chord deep inside Bayla. Yes, their precious children were so pure.

"Now listen to this: It also says there that when *Mashiach* comes, their Rebbe is not allowed to stop the learning to take the children to watch the construction of the *Beis HaMikdash*! Isn't that amazing? He can only take them to see it when they've finished their regular day of learning."

Bayla suddenly remembered that she had to leave in another five minutes but she dared not say what was on her mind. She had learned the hard way that timing was crucial in relationships.

"Bayla," said Miriam dramatically, her voice rising a notch, "do you realize what this means?"

"Miriam, my dear friend," Bayla said with a smile, "why don't you calm down and tell me, okay?"

"It means, Bayla, that every single thing I did this morning would be just the same even when *Mashiach* is here. I'll still be making lunches, packing school bags, waiting for the bus — don't you see Bayla? Of course, I imagine we'll feel different, closer to Hashem, but our priorities right now will be the same. When I'm packing lunches, if I hear that *Mashiach* has arrived, I have to finish those lunches first because my children's Torah takes priority. It says it right there in the Gemara! There's no such thing as a mundane activity when you care for a Jewish child."

There was a pause while the words hung in the air.

"Miriam," Bayla finally said, "Hashem blessed me when He gave you to me for a friend. Do you mean to tell me that when the *Beis HaMikdash* is rebuilt the children can't go and watch until *cheder* is finished for the day?"

"That's right, Bayla. That's exactly what I mean to tell you. My husband told me that Reish Lakish says in the name of Rabbi Yehudah HaNasi, 'The world endures only in the merit of yeshivah children,' and that one is not allowed to interrupt the Torah study of yeshivah children even for the building of the *Beis HaMikdash*."

It was an ordinary moment in time, one like thousands of others. But Bayla and Miriam elevated it. They spoke no politics, no weather, no talk about the sales at the malls.

As they sat there watching their children play, they had the deep satisfaction of really knowing that what they were doing with their lives was the most important thing they could ever be doing. They did not have to go anywhere to know it. All they had to do was cultivate an appreciation for the blessings they had in their own homes.

For the Sake of Peace

✐ Tuition

In this world, Mrs. Bluma Wallach was never rich or famous. But the mitzvos she did, quietly, and often without anyone knowing exactly how she did them, built a shining palace for her in the world of truth. Here is an example of an "ordinary woman" responding to the mitzvah opportunities that presented themselves at the threshold of her home.

Mrs. Wallach's charity fund lacked rich patrons. It was the monthly five- and ten-dollar donations from friends of Mama (as she was fondly called) that kept it going. And a friend, in Mama's dictionary, was anyone with whom she came into contact long enough to tell them about her fund.

Mama's house was tiny. But that didn't stop her from receiving all guests graciously. One of these was Bayla, a young Bais Yaakov student from a non-religious home who lived in the neighborhood. She was a regular visitor.

One afternoon, Bayla arrived on Mrs. Wallach's doorstep in tears. In the past, Bayla's parents had never interfered with their daughter's religious observance, but now she had reached the legal age of employment and they insisted that she leave school to go out to work. Bayla, however, had her heart set on continuing her education at the Teachers Seminary. It didn't take Mama long to size up the situation. She set Bayla to work peeling potatoes in the kitchen, ran to her neighbor's phone (she didn't own one), and got to work.

That night, Mrs. Finkelstein, the principal of Bayla's Bais Yaakov, paid Mrs. Wallach a visit. They sat at the kitchen table enjoying tea and cookies. "It's really a shame," sighed the principal. "Bayla is one of our top students. She would have made an excellent teacher."

"Excuse me," said Mrs. Wallach, "but who said she's not going into teaching?"

"I thought you knew that her parents insist on sending her out to work," the principal said. "Actually, I thought that was why you invited me over — to try to smooth things out."

"Nothing of the sort, Mrs. Finkelstein. I called you to give you this." With that, Mama pulled an envelope full of money from her apron pocket. "Here is tuition for the next six months. Bayla will stay in school and, G-d willing, she will go to the Teachers Seminary. Don't you worry. I will speak with her parents this evening."

The principal stood up, her facial expression one of amazement. "Thank you so much! You can't imagine how many people will benefit from this generosity. She is a very gifted girl, you know, and will make a fine teacher."

It was always a mystery to Mrs. Wallach's family just exactly how she managed to do it, but for the next two and a half years, Bayla's tuition was paid in full.

And that's not the end of the story.

Bayla's *parents* received a monthly stipend as well. It was a sum equivalent to what Bayla would have earned had she gone to work. Mama made sure to bring it herself without fail, on the first of each month.

Epilogue: Bayla just made a bar mitzvah for her second oldest son. Not surprisingly, Mama attended. When she went over to congratulate the proud grandparents, Bayla's mother said, "You know, Mrs. Wallach, all those years ago when you paid

my daughter's tuition, I was very angry with you. I felt you had no right to meddle in our lives. But my hands were tied — because every month, like clockwork, you brought the 'salary.' Now, on this special day, I must ask your forgiveness." Her eyes filled with tears. "I have one unmarried son on the West Coast and my other daughter is living in an ashram in India. But, thanks to you, Mrs. Wallach, from my Bayla I have true nachas."

A Fair Share

No one can take away what really belongs to us. Although in our times the channels for parnasah often seem very convoluted and complex, it is all determined by Heaven, not by our own hand. With her simple faith, the wife in this contemporary episode demonstrated a tenacious belief in this principle. Besides the avoidance of unnecessary aggravation, she was rewarded with an unexpected bonus.

Eli Sussman had been working as a computer salesman for seven years when he was advised to leave and set up his own company. He had learned a tremendous amount about the business from his employer, the store owner, in those seven years, and he enjoyed the work, but his financial situation was such that he could no longer remain at the same salary level.

The first few months went very smoothly. Then suddenly, without prior warning, he received a very angry phone call from his former boss. He accused Eli of stealing customers and unfairly setting lower prices, and even went so far as to threaten him with a lawsuit if he didn't compensate him for the lost income. Eli spoke to his Rav and a lawyer who both advised him to go to court. After all, he had done nothing improper. Why should he pay a former employer just because the man felt he had lost out?

Logic said fight, but his wife's intuition made her say to her husband, "No. Money comes from Hashem. Let's give him the money he feels he deserves. If it truly belongs to us, Hashem will give it back."

Things were difficult that first year, but they managed. Gradually Eli paid his former boss the money he demanded. At the same time, he developed a substantial clientele who proceeded to recommend him to an even broader circle of friends, relatives and neighbors.

Shortly after Rosh Hashanah, he was surprised by a call from his former employer. Unfortunately, the man had slipped and broken his leg and had no one he could trust to keep his firm operating while he recuperated. One part-time employee had recently moved and had not yet been replaced, while the full-time assistant was on vacation. If Eli would not lend a helping hand, he would have to close the store, which would mean a sizable loss of income. He offered to pay Eli at least double the regular salary for a five-hour shift each day for two weeks.

Eli felt it was an opportunity to restore goodwill between them while earning some extra money which he could always put to good use. After the two weeks, he came home with his paycheck. "Do you remember when we discussed whether or not to go to court?" he asked his wife with a smile. "Your words came true. Here it is, almost to the exact penny. Everything I paid in compensation, Hashem put right back into my hand."

He Left Her at the Bus Station

From time to time, Rebbetzin Tzivia Chadash (see pgs. 119-128) suffered from attacks of severe rheumatism. For relief, she sometimes traveled to the hot springs in Teveryah. There, she could relax for a few days, and take treatments. But even when she was concerned with her own needs, Rebbetzin Tzivia's mind was always set on helping others.

In the small hotel where they stayed, there was a newly divorced young woman. The woman sat there looking downcast, picking on her food, not really eating. But Rebbetzin Tzivia was not one to wait for anyone to ask for help. It was as if she had a special eye to spot other people's suffering and a special heart which enabled others to share their burdens with her.

In the course of their conversation, the young woman revealed to the Rebbetzin that she was very unhappy about her divorce. "The truth is," she said bitterly, "I don't even remember how it happened. One thing led to another and before we really knew what was happening, we were filing for divorce. Now he's living in Ra'anana."

The Rebbetzin gently coaxed the ex-husband's name and place of residence out of the distraught woman, and on the way home from her trip to the Teveryah hot springs she took action. When the bus pulled into Ra'anana, the Rebbetzin turned to her husband and said, "Please, you continue on with the luggage, and I'll be home *b'ezras Hashem* in a few hours." The Rav knew what she was up to. "It's all right. I'll take the luggage. May Hashem make you successful."

She got off the bus and went to find the woman's former

husband. Within the hour, she was in his tiny apartment. She found him in a very sad and depressed state. "What did I do?" he told her in a choking voice. "I threw out my good wife."

Rebbetzin Tzivia told him, "You know, your wife is also very sad and upset. She wants to marry you again but she is afraid you won't want her back. Why don't you make a fresh start? You can stay in our home. I will contact your wife and we will see what she says."

Within a few weeks the couple had remarried. They were very happy, like newlyweds. They kept saying, "What was wrong with us? Why did we quarrel over such silly things?"

Today, whenever someone from Rebbetzin Tzivia's family hears someone say, "It's not my business, I don't have to get involved, it's not polite," they think of their mother and stories such as this one. She never thought it wasn't her business. And look at what she accomplished!

✑ Reversing the Charges

*Y*ossi had always been close with his grandmother, who was a feisty, high-spirited individual. One example of her outgoing personality was demonstrated during World War II when she and her husband went to apply for their United States citizenship papers. When it was grandmother's turn to be questioned, the examiner asked, "In what merit do you feel you deserve to be an American citizen?"

She responded, "Sir, I have a son in uniform overseas fighting the enemy. That's my merit. Where is *your* uniform?"

They got their papers.

Without benefit of a religious upbringing, Yossi began a search after graduating college that eventually led him to yeshivah. No matter what changes he made in his lifestyle, the weekly phone call to his grandmother remained a constant.

Like many contemporary families, theirs was no more than a few generations removed from true Yiddishkeit. When Yossi became religious, his grandmother always told him, "*Mein tatte* is very proud of his *einekel*."

Yossi did whatever he could to maintain close ties with his family who, in turn, always had a liberal, easygoing policy with their children. When Yossi would go to visit his married brother, for example, he'd say, "Yossi, you can set the house up any way you need to for Shabbos. Don't worry, we won't touch a thing." And that's exactly what would happen. Even the children were told, "Those are Uncle Yossi's Shabbos lights. We can't touch them until Saturday night."

Because of the good relationship with his family and their warm acceptance of his new lifestyle, Yossi was particularly upset when he found out that his sister's wedding would take place in a "universalist temple." He didn't want to spoil family togetherness, but how could he attend such a wedding?

He decided to consult a major Torah personality.

Yossi walked into the Rabbi's house with a heavy heart and not without a little trepidation. After all, he had never before been in the presence of such an illustrious Torah sage.

"*Shalom aleichem*," the Rabbi greeted him with a warm smile. "Please have a seat."

Yossi looked into the twinkling brown eyes gazing intently at him from across the table and instantly relaxed. Feeling as if he were talking to a true friend, he proceeded to explain his predicament. "My baby sister is getting married in six weeks."

"Mazel tov!" said the sage. "May she merit to build a *bayis ne'eman b'Yisrael*."

"Amen, thank you, but actually," said Yossi, urgency in his voice, "I'm in a very problematic situation. My sister and I have always had a very strong and close relationship. Five years ago, I entered yeshivah to learn. I became totally observant. My family has always been very respectful of my choices.

"But my problem, Rabbi, is that everything at the wedding will be *treif*. The food will be *treif*, there will be mixed dancing, the ceremony will be held in what's called an 'interfaith temple' because her fiance is a heart specialist and he teaches a kind of stress-reduction based on Eastern meditation. He's a Jew but he calls himself a 'spiritual universalist' and he refuses to have a Jewish ceremony. Rabbi, what can I do?"

The Rabbi sighed and held his head in his hands for a few minutes while Yossi waited nervously for an answer. When the sage lifted his head, his face was wet with tears.

"Can't you ask this question of someone else? What can I tell you? I can't tell you to go. May Hashem bless you to be successful in everything you do and be patient. *B'ezras Hashem* it should be for *simchahs* that peace will be restored to your family."

"Amen," answered Yossi. Feeling broken and close to tears himself, he left the study.

The winter air was cold and refreshing. As he walked back to his dormitory he thought back to the years when he and his sister were just a couple of kids. Various scenes flashed through his mind: the time he was pushing her on the swing, teasing her about being scared to go higher; the handmade birthday card she had given him one year; how he taught her to play the guitar. And now he wouldn't be attending her wedding.

He had tried so hard to make sure that his becoming religious wouldn't drive a wedge between him and his family. He dreaded calling them to tell them that he wouldn't be there but figured he might as well get it over with.

As expected, the news wasn't well received. Yossi clung to the Rabbi's words that perhaps with patience and his own *simchahs*, the family would come together again.

What totally caught him by surprise was his next phone call.

"Yossi," his roommate called from the hallway, "you have a phone call."

"Coming," Yossi called back as a feeling of dread welled up in his heart. *I wonder who could be calling me now?* he thought.

It was his grandmother. She came right to the point. "What do you mean you're not coming to Tanie's wedding?"

Oh boy, here we go. She's never, ever called me before. What can I say?

Yossi stood there speechless with the phone in his hand, staring blankly at the receiver.

"*Nu?* You can't come to say a mazel tov to your sister?!"

Suddenly, it was as though an angel stood next to Yossi whispering in his ear. "*Mein tatte* is very proud of his *einekel.*"

"Bubbie," he heard himself asking, "would your father have gone to a wedding like that?"

There was silence at the other end. Suddenly his grandmother burst out, "*Mein tatte* was a *chassid* and a *groiser tzaddik*! You're right, *mein kinde* — you stay there in New York with those real Rabbis!"

Yossi hung up the phone elated. He knew that if he had gotten through to his grandmother it would have an effect on the rest of the family.

Four months later, the Rabbi's words of blessing came true: Yossi was getting married. Three weeks before the wedding, he received a phone call.

"Hello, Yossi. It's Tanie. I called to find out, I mean, mazel tov, and I wanted to know how long my sleeves have to be at your wedding."

Yossi was speechless — and this time, out of happiness. "Tanie, please forgive me. I know you were very hurt that I couldn't be there."

"Grandma told us we couldn't be mad at you because you're named after her father and he was a *tzaddik*. She told us that if he were alive, he wouldn't have come to my wedding either! She also said we should be happy to have someone like you who is bringing the Torah back to our family. You should have heard her, Yossi! She's so proud of you."

Three weeks later, at Yossi's wedding, the family was brought together for a true simchah.

Saving Lives

~ Muma Sarah

They called her Muma Sarah (Aunt Sarah). To support Torah and mitzvos in Communist Russia, she would disguise herself as a peasant and travel the countryside smuggling considerable amounts of money to the underground yeshivos. She obtained false identity papers for hundreds of chassidim, as well as for Rebbetzin Chanah Schneerson, the mother of the late Lubavitcher Rebbe, zt"l. Widowed tragically at the age of 47, she nonetheless carried on, fearless and undaunted by the challenge of the life-threatening work. Typically, Muma Sarah refused to make use of the official documents she had prepared for herself. "When there is no one left to help," she declared, "then I will leave." The following vignettes take us back in time to a behind-the-Iron-Curtain era that fortunately no longer exists. The valor of the heroine, though, is timeless.

Born on the 26th of Tishrei in 1891, in Rudniya, White Russia, Muma Sarah was the daughter of Reb Ben-Zion Raskin. During that era, a Jew did not need a visionary's eyes to know that his children were in grave spiritual danger. Reb Raskin was known to have one request constantly in his heart and on his lips: That even in the wasteland of Communist Russia, his offspring would be *"erliche Yidden,"* G-d-fearing, observant Jews. He would beg his Rebbes for their prayers and blessings that the spiritual lineage of his family remain unblemished. Although it was a rare phenomenon in those days, Reb Raskin's request was granted; not a single one of his children or grandchildren went astray. Beyond that, Hashem blessed him with a daughter whose great and noble soul was entirely given over to saving others.

Muma Sarah was trained from a very young age to sacrifice her comfort for mitzvos. The door to her childhood home stood open day and night. She would often be awakened from sleep to give her bed to a weary traveler or an unexpected guest.

In 1909, at the age of 18, Sarah married Reb Michael, the son of Reb Yehoshua Katzenelenbogen, the *ba'al koreh* (Torah reader) in Lubavitch on Rosh Hashanah. At her *chupah*, (wedding) the young Sarah wore a *sheitel*, (wig) an extremely rare occurrence in those days.

After the wedding, the couple spent three years in Lubavitch, where Sarah worked in the kitchen of the Yeshivah Tomchei Temimim. During this time she had the opportunity to form a close friendship with Rebbetzin Shterna Sarah, the wife of the Rebbe Rashab. Sarah would go to *shul* with the Rebbetzin and would *daven* alongside her near the other women of the Rebbe's family, including his mother, Rebbetzin Rivkah.

In the early 1900s in White Russia, Torah study was illegal and dangerous. A harsh fate awaited the teacher or student who was caught by the ever-watchful agents of the KGB. But a mother who knows her purpose in life knows that sending her children to a state-run school, designed to inculcate atheism and hatred of religion, is far worse than death. For Muma Sarah, the choice was between living death and eternal life. Thus each day she would take her children to the hidden *cheder* where they learned to cleave to the Creator through the Torah, His Tree of Life.

But Muma Sarah also knew that transmitting Torah requires living role models. Therefore, at tremendous expense and at the risk of being found out by the authorities, Muma Sarah took in and supported five yeshivah *bachurim* for approximately five years. She was so worried about her children's *chinuch* that she provided them with an in-house community of living examples of how a Jew should *daven*, learn, and conduct himself in daily life.

In 1938, right after Simchas Torah, the secret police came to the Katzenelenbogen home after midnight and dragged R' Michael, Muma Sarah's husband, away. Sarah was 47 years old; she never saw her husband again. Another woman in a similar situation might have given in to despair, but Muma Sarah found the courage and determination to continue her devoted efforts on behalf of her people. In the days immediately following her husband's arrest (and unbeknownst to her, his subsequent execution) Sarah packed up her two older sons' belongings and sent the boys to study in the clandestine yeshivah in Leningrad. To her mind, this was simply the way it had to be. Any other course of action was virtually inconceivable. Two years later, one of these sons was arrested and sentenced to five years in prison.

During this time she approached the wife of Reb Elchonon Shagolow. He had been arrested at the same time as Muma Sarah's husband. According to family tradition, Sarah said to her, "Our husbands are sitting behind bars together (she was unaware that both had been executed); let us join our families through marriage!"

An astute and successful businesswoman who dealt in

fabrics and the illegal slaughter and sale of kosher meat, Sarah consistently donated large sums to the underground yeshivah movement. She also volunteered to act as an intercity courier to transfer funds from yeshivah to yeshivah. This was dangerous work, as the KGB would conduct random searches on trains and at the stations.

During one of her frequent trips, the carriage she was riding in broke down. Sarah walked to a nearby inn where she could wait until the necessary repairs were made. Reb Peretz Mockin, an expert *mohel*, was traveling on the same carriage and he also decided to take shelter in the inn. Suddenly, a man burst in, ran up to Reb Peretz and whispered, "My wife gave birth to a boy. We need a *mohel*. Can you give me any advice?" Reb Peretz smiled at the Divine grace that rested on them even in such dark times. "You have a *mohel* right here, my son," he answered, "come, we mustn't waste any time."

Sarah rushed to a nearby drugstore and bought the essentials for the *bris*. Reb Peretz performed a speedy *bris*, with Sarah as the *sandek*. Afterwards, they made it back to the carriage just in time to continue the journey.

On another trip, Muma Sarah, dressed as a simple Russian peasant, was traveling to visit her son Shimon, who had been arrested and was awaiting deportation to Siberia. On the way, she met a young yeshivah student who was fleeing the police. She recognized him immediately but when she approached, his face blanched with panic. "Don't worry," she whispered in Yiddish, "I'm in disguise. What do you need?"

With a mixture of relief and gratitude, the young man explained his predicament. "I'm running away. The KGB is after me and I don't have a train ticket. I have money, but I'm afraid if I stand in line to buy a ticket, they'll catch me."

After listening intently and thinking for a minute, Muma Sarah answered, "Don't worry. Board the train with me and make sure you stay right next to me."

The two of them got on the train together. Once it began to move, Muma Sarah, in her Russian babushka and simple dress, took out her ticket and held it in front of her. She pretended to be very proud of her ticket and made a great show of it, studying it intently. She put it away and took it out again, looked at the other passengers and pointed dramatically to her ticket with a wide, happy smile on her face.

Continuing her act, she went from one person to the next amongst her fellow passengers, waving her ticket in their faces. "My good people, you all see that I have a ticket, right?" She did this over and over again, going up and down the moving car, until people were sure that they were traveling with a simple and somewhat childlike peasant woman.

Some time later, the conductor walked through the car shouting, "Tickets! Tickets!" All the passengers took out their tickets and handed them to the conductor for marking. Sarah stood close to the *bachur* and surreptitiously passed him her ticket. She then quietly drifted away. When the boy's turn came, he showed the ticket to the conductor who then marked it.

When the conductor reached Sarah and asked her for her ticket she murmured, "Yes, my ticket … of course I have a ticket," and began rummaging through her bags, pulling out their contents and making quite a scene of her search. Turning to her fellow passengers, she asked them to bear witness to the fact that she did, in fact, have a ticket. "I can't understand it!" she wailed in mock dismay. "I had my ticket only a moment ago — you all saw it! Now it's gone. Please, my good people, tell the gentleman that you saw I had a ticket."

A chorus of voices readily responded assuring the conductor that the poor lady did indeed have a ticket that she must have misplaced. The conductor accepted their testimony, shrugged his shoulders and said, "It's all right. I believe you."

In 1946, the opportunity arose for many Chabad chassidim to escape Russia through the use of forged Polish papers. A committee was formed to run this operation. If one member was found out and arrested, someone else would come forward to take his place. Sarah was a member of the committee. She was personally responsible for procuring hundreds of false documents for people in the community as well as for herself and her entire family. But her own papers were to come last. Like many of those upon whom greatness is bestowed, she could not endure a moment's rest knowing others were suffering.

One of the people she helped was Rebbetzin Chanah Schneerson, the mother of the Lubavitcher Rebbe, *zt"l*. The Rebbetzin arrived in Moscow from Alma Ata very frightened because the name Schneerson was known and immediately suspect. Muma Sarah was adamant about the proper course of action. She convinced the Rebbetzin to join the illegal exodus, personally making the arrangements for her own son and his wife to travel with the Rebbetzin and care for her during the long and difficult trip that took them across the border to Poland, Germany, and finally France. Sarah accompanied them to Lemberg, right near the Polish border. There she gave the Rebbetzin the documents that she had been saving for herself. It was impossible for her to bring herself to cross the border when so many people were still in grave danger.

Upon her return, the Russian authorities discovered the illegal escape route. The committee organizers were hunted down and arrested. Sarah managed to elude the dragnet, but she was now a wanted criminal, with her picture posted in every police station throughout the country.

One of the other organizers, known for his courageous and feisty spirit, Reb Mendel Futerfas, was caught and given a 20-year sentence. News of this reached Sarah. She knew that a prisoner could not survive in the labor camp system without money to bribe guards and wardens. The question was how she was going to smuggle such a large sum of money to Reb Mendel, who was in jail awaiting deportation to a camp.

A very simple solution came to mind, but one that required tremendous courage, nerve and daring. Sarah went to the tailor and bought a very warm man's winter coat. She painstakingly opened up the lining and created an inner lining — of currency. Then she meticulously re-sewed the lining so that the alteration was undetectable. Finally, she set out for the lion's den.

Arriving at the prison, Sarah explained to the guard that a close relative of hers was being deported. She requested permission to see him one last time to give him a coat to keep him warm in the frozen wasteland of the camp. The guard granted her request and motioned her to sign the visitor's registry. Ever wary, she scrawled one of her seven aliases.

When Reb Mendel saw Sarah enter his cell, accompanied by a prison escort, he nearly fell off his cot. He tried to make Sarah aware of the fact that there was a warrant out for her arrest and that she was in tremendous danger. Sarah calmed him down, handed him the coat, and made a quick exit. By the time the prison authorities realized who their visitor was, Sarah was miles away.

Years later, after Reb Mendel had been freed and was living in England, he would tell the story about the coat's inner lining many times. The money in that coat had indeed saved his life.

On her way to visit one of her sons, Muma Sarah sent him a telegram announcing her arrival and asking to be met at the train station. What she did not know was that his house was under surveillance. The KGB intercepted the telegram, read it, and then allowed it to be delivered to her son. Her son sent an older couple to meet his mother at the train station and to warn her not to come to the house. But by then it was too late. The one who had freed so many others was not to be free herself. The KGB agent pretended to be a porter and offered to help her with her suitcases. He escorted her to a waiting car and drove directly to the KGB's building. The older couple never had a chance to warn Sarah. They were immediately arrested, as were Sarah's son and the person who picked up the telegram.

At the trial, they were each tried for various "crimes" including not informing the authorities of illegal exit activities, and hosting prayer-group gatherings in their homes. Muma Sarah was accused of a number of different "crimes" until they reached her worst offense: wanting to leave Russia and go to Israel. The penalty: death.

After her death sentence was handed down, when her turn came to speak, instead of weeping and begging for mercy, she declared, "I am happy and grateful to the

Almighty that He enabled me to smuggle my children and so many others out of Russia so that they could be free to live as Torah-observant Jews."

Sarah then walked over to her son to comfort him. "Be strong in your faith. Don't worry about me. G-d willing, you will get out."

Although she was given a chance to appeal the death penalty, Sarah waited for the appeal in solitary confinement on death row. After two months in solitary confinement, her sentence was reduced to "only" 25 years. They transferred her from death row to the general prison. Men and women were separated, with women on the lower level and male prisoners on the upper.

Always a mother, Sarah somehow devised ways to communicate with her son. As the guard made his rounds from one end of the floor to the other, Sarah's son would write a note, tie it to the end of a thread, and weight it down on a crust of bread. Holding one end of the thread, he would lower the note to the floor below, while banging on the floor. The pounding on the ceiling would signal Sarah to go out and look for a note.

Sarah would take the note, read it quickly, write an answer, and hook it on the thread to be raised back up. She had to do this in less than a minute since that was how long it took the guard to make his rounds. For the most part, aside from asking about her son's health, most of her notes were questions of halachah: What should she do about *davening*? The only *Shemoneh Esrei* she knew by heart was *Minchah* of Shabbos ... That was what was on her mind in the prison cell.

Shortly before Pesach, Muma Sarah's son, who was due to be sent away to a labor camp, requested permission to see his mother. A visit was granted, yet the deep happiness of their reunion was marred by the clouds of an unknown future. Even here, in the depths of a Soviet prison, Muma Sarah did not greet her son empty-handed. As she walked in, she held a small bag in each hand. They were filled with sugar cubes. Each day she had set them aside from her meager portion of sugar cubes so that her son would be able to have the precious source of energy over Pesach.

Within 24 hours of their meeting, he was called in by the director of the prison. His facial expression stern, the head warden handed the prisoner a package. Inside were his mother's clothes. On the ninth of Nissan, He Who releases the bound took the soul of Muma Sarah from the Russian prison. She had suffered a heart attack and died.

Muma Sarah left her children and descendants a legacy of *mesiras nefesh* and *ahavas Yisrael*, as well as *kiddush Hashem*.

Although Muma Sarah passed away in a solitary-confinement prison cell, her efforts on behalf of the Jewish people continue to bear fruit for generations. Today, all of Muma Sarah's descendants, her children, grandchildren, great-grandchildren and great-great-grandchildren, are *bnei Torah*, dedicating their lives to the values and ideals handed down by the dynasty of Chabad Rebbes. Her offspring can be found in America, Australia, Brazil, England, Israel, and South Africa, contributing in major ways to building up communities in *Klal Yisrael*.

One of Muma Sarah's granddaughters, who lives in Tzefas, often gives talks about her noble and courageous grandmother. "When I speak to groups of women about my grandmother's life, it awakens within me a very deep yearning to have known her. I feel that it is a big *z'chus* and tremendous responsibility to be a descendant of such a person. I try to instill in my children those qualities of *ahavas Yisrael* and *mesiras nefesh* for which she gave her life."

The Heavenly Court

Rabbi Shimon Bar Yochai had free access to *Gan Eden* in his lifetime, the Midrash tells us. Whenever he wanted some information, he would take a walk in front of the heavenly gates, waiting for two angels to come out. They would ask him what he wanted, and then reveal whatever secrets he wished to know.

"I would like to know," he once asked the angels, "what reward awaits righteous women."

"Wait until we enter and ask the *Rosh Yeshivah* in *Gan Eden*," they answered, for they did not know the answer themselves. They returned with a message: "Follow us and we will take you to the women's palaces, which we have never seen before."

They walked until they came to the palaces, each one built on a higher level than the one before. The higher the palace, the more spiritual a place it was, explained the angels. The first two palaces were reserved for righteous women who had been through hellfire for purification, although they were surely considered *tzidkaniyos*. The next four were reserved for women who had never required the purification process.

Batya, daughter of Pharaoh, presided over the first palace, which contained tens of thousands of souls of worthy women who had raised and provided for poor Jewish children. Every soul enjoyed its own measure of spiritual pleasure, light and honor. Three times a day a heavenly voice would come to announce the visit of Moshe Rabbeinu. This was the signal for Batya to enter a curtained partition from where she could gaze upon Moshe Rabbeinu's countenance. And each time she would exclaim, "Fortunate am I for having a share in the upbringing of such a luminous being." She would then bow and return to the other souls in that palace.

The souls appeared just as the women did in their lifetimes, clothed with raiments of light, garments similar to those the men wore, except that the men's were brighter, reflecting the Torah that they study.

Batya taught Torah to the women in her section, explaining the reasons for mitzvos, particularly those applying to women. The souls here were called "the serene women."

The second palace was presided over by Serach, the daughter of Asher, and also contained thousands of worthy women who in their lifetime tended to the old and infirm. Similarly, Serach bas Asher cared for her grandfather, Yaakov, and revived his mourning soul by telling him that Yosef was still alive. In this palace, announcements were made thrice daily, calling attention to the visits of Yosef HaTzaddik. Upon hearing them, Serach would retire to a partitioned area to gaze upon his holy face, each time exclaiming anew, "How fortunate I am to have had the privilege of telling my grandfather Yaakov the good news of Yosef, thereby restoring his Divine inspiration." The rest of the time she taught Torah to the women in her palace and together they praised Hashem.

The third palace was presided over by Yocheved, and

contained the souls of women who, like Yocheved, were fortunate in bearing righteous children. Yocheved would gather them thrice daily to recite the Song of the Sea. She and her daughter would lead the singing. When they would come to the verse, "And Miriam the prophetess took the timbrels ..." even the heavenly angels would join in their rejoicing.

The fourth palace, the highest and most important of all, was presided over by Devorah the prophetess. It contained the souls of women of distinction who were leaders or exceptional personalities. They helped Devorah sing her song each day and were aided as well by the heavenly angels in their praises to Hashem.

There were four more deeply hidden palaces for the four matriarchs which no eye has yet beheld. Each midnight the souls would come forth to bask in a brilliant light, after which they would return to their palaces (from *Tales of the Heavenly Court* by Yisrael Yaakov Klapholtz, translated by Sheindel Weinbach).

Send My Husband Anywhere — as Long as It's Eretz Yisrael!

Rebbetzin Tzivia (see stories pgs. 99 and 122) came to Eretz Yisrael as a young girl in 1925. Her uncle, a Rosh Yeshivah, arranged a shidduch for her with one of his talmidim. At that time, an international wedding didn't mean faxes, e-mailed menus, and discount flights. It meant, quite simply, overwhelming loneliness, sacrifices and resolve.

From one week after the wedding until her death over 60 years later, the home she and her husband established was always open, 24 hours a day. Whether it involved cooking for many people, making up extra beds at two in the morning, or keeping a ready supply of coffee, tea and cookies near the huge custom-made copper samovar for the yeshivah boys, Rebbetzin Tzivia always answered her husband's requests for more guests with one word: "Good." Therefore it was surprising and puzzling to all when she refused a request by European gedolim that her husband return to open a new yeshivah there. Her daughter, herself a prominent Rebbetzin in Yerushalayim today, tells this story.

My mother, Rebbetzin Tzivia, of blessed memory, was born in Lita to European parents. Things were very different then. For one, people didn't travel back and forth frequently. Letters often failed to arrive and there were no telephones. By the time my brother was almost three and I was one and a half, it had been quite a few years since my mother had seen her parents. We were the only grandchildren and she longed to give her parents the *nachas* of seeing us. So, although it was terribly expensive and pre-war ocean travel was often dangerous, my mother took us to Tel Aviv and we boarded a ship sailing to Europe. Imagine it: One woman with two toddlers and her suitcases. My mother said that she put us on leashes to make sure we wouldn't run away and fall overboard! When the ship docked, tired as we were, we had to make a five-hour journey by train and then by coach to reach our destination. But my mother always felt very happy that she had made such an effort, especially since shortly after this visit her father passed away.

HaRav Chadash, *zt"l*, my father, was a *mashgiach* in Chevron Yeshivah in Yerushalayim. A few months before we left to visit my mother's parents, several *gedolim* in Europe sent my father a telegram asking him to come back and open a large yeshivah in Warsaw. My father seriously considered accepting their offer. But when he sat down with my mother to discuss it, she said, "You know, I suffered so much until I finally came to *Eretz Yisrael*. At first, I was so lonely. After that, we lived through the Chevron massacre. Now finally, *baruch Hashem*, we are here in Yerushalayim. After all that, how can I turn around and go back to Europe? I want to stay here in *Eretz Yisrael*."

Then, shortly after we arrived for our visit in Europe, the Chafetz Chaim, *zt"l*, passed away. Rebbetzin Tzivia's father had been very close to him, so naturally my mother went to the *levayah*. Afterwards, a messenger came to tell her that the *gedolim* wished to speak with her.

When she went inside the study, they asked her directly, "Why do you refuse to agree to your husband's coming here? It is very important."

She had very firm convictions about her husband teaching Torah and raising a family in *Eretz Yisrael*. Many years later she told me that she also had terrible premonitions about what was to come. She answered the Rabbis, "*Eretz Yisrael* is a desert when it comes to Yiddishkeit. There are hardly any yeshivos. If you want to open a yeshivah in *Eretz Yisrael*, even if it is at the farthest end of the land in some tiny town, I will go. But not here in Europe on this foreign soil. Can't you feel that the ground is already burning under your feet?"

Only a short while later, Europe was indeed engulfed in

the flames of the Holocaust. After World War II, when Rabbi Chizkiyahu Mishkofsky, one of the aforementioned Rabbis, escaped to *Eretz Yisrael*, he came to our home and said to my mother, "Rebbetzin Tzivia, you were right!"

Rav Chadash, my father, always told his children that he was alive because of their mother. She saved her family's lives when she refused to go back. She told as many people as she could, "Come to Israel, the ground is already burning in Europe." Everyone who listened to her was saved.

❧ *Portrait of a Home: Chevron — Yerushalayim*

Rebbetzin Tzivia Chadash, z"l, left Europe as a young girl to come to Eretz Yisrael. Her uncle, HaRav Moshe Mordechai Epstein, zt"l, was the Rosh Yeshivah of Chevron Yeshivah, located at that time in Chevron. She was his sister's daughter and, as her guardian, he made her shidduch with HaRav Chadash, then a talmid in the Yeshivah and later its mashgiach for 60 years.

Rebbetzin Tzivia would tell her daughter (wife of HaRav Ezrachi, shlita, of Yeshivas Ateres Yisrael in Bayit Vegan, see previous story) vivid stories of those early years. Here Rebbetzin Ezrachi shares some of her family memories, giving us a verbal portrait of her mother's early life in Chevron and the family's subsequent move to Yerushalayim. Once again, we discover the oft-forgotten truth that great people worked hard to achieve their greatness.

My father was HaRav Chadash, *zt"l*, *mashgiach* of Chevron Yeshivah for 60 years. He was like a father to the *bachurim*. As soon as they set foot in the yeshivah, they knew that they had a home.

Our home was open day and night. The *bachurim* would come and take coffee, tea and biscuits — whatever they wanted. For most of them, it was the only place of refuge from their loneliness. In those days it was impossible to travel home frequently. So the *bachurim* came and stayed and that was it. Their deep longing for a home was filled in my parents' home.

My parents were married in the summer of 1928. None of the family came from Europe to the wedding. My father had a brother learning in the yeshivah as did my mother. The only people at the wedding were these two brothers, the *Rosh Yeshivah's* family, and the *bachurim*.

My parents rented an apartment with a shared kitchen. The first Shabbos after their marriage they were invited to the *Rosh Yeshivah's* home. The very next Shabbos my father told my mother that he had some friends who very much wanted to come and eat with them. And she agreed. After being married only three weeks, my father asked if they could have 30 *bachurim* for the Rosh Hashanah meals. My mother was a young girl, far away from her family. Loneliness was a basic part of her day. She understood that the *bachurim* were longing for a home. Her answer then was the same as it was for their entire married life together. It was always one word: "Good."

Although they had barely any money and she was not accustomed to cooking vegetables, let alone for 30 people, my mother learned quickly. She had a neighbor from the Old Yishuv in Yerushalayim who taught her how to cook many dishes with vegetables, the main food available then. She became quite a skilled *balabusta*.

Seudah shelishis was one of her favorite times. The *bachurim* would come and sing for hours. The sky would gradually turn dark and Shabbos would long since be over, but the *bachurim*, many of whom went on to become renowned Rebbeim in Klal Yisrael, stayed and sang.

In 1929 my parents suffered a terrible tragedy — the Black Shabbos. The Arabs went from house to house in Chevron, killing Jews. Somehow, my family survived. My mother's neighbor, the one she shared the kitchen with, was killed right before her eyes. Covered with her neighbor's blood, my mother quickly lay down on the floor and pretended that she was dead. When the Arabs saw her saturated with blood they beat her to make sure she wasn't still alive. Despite her terror and her intense pain, she did not scream or move a muscle.

My father was also part of a group of men who pretended to be dead. Somehow the Arabs never went back to check on them. Twenty-four of the yeshivah's *bachurim* were killed, may Hashem avenge the death of these holy martyrs. After that, the yeshivah moved to Yerushalayim.

Even more *bachurim* came to the yeshivah in Yerushalayim. And again, my mother's house became their home. No samovar was available that was large enough to serve all the guests they had every week. My mother had to have a huge copper one custom-made. On Shabbos, that samovar, filled with hot water, stood in the kitchen. Next to it under the table was a large basket of cookies. Nearby, also in baskets, were sugar, coffee and tea. My mother would tell us to finish our meal quickly because the *bachurim* were waiting outside. Even after the young men married and were sent to different parts of *Eretz Yisrael*, they would often come back to the yeshivah to be with us for Shabbos.

But our house wasn't full only on Shabbos. Everyone

knew that at any time of the day or night, our door was open. As soon as someone came to our doorstep, he was no longer a stranger. My mother was ready to help in any way she could.

Every Rosh Hashanah my parents made a large *Kiddush*. People came from all over. My brother and I would leave *shul* a little early to prepare while our mother stayed to see if she had missed any new faces. Once, for instance, she saw a young girl who had recently arrived from Holland. The Rabbi there had been one of our students and now he had gone to help people after the war. He had told this young woman, "All you need to know is the address of Chevron Yeshivah in Yerushalayim. Just go there and Rebbetzin Chadash will take care of you." She told us the story later. My mother smiled and said, "So come to us!" The girl had no family in the country and my mother took her in and made her part of our extended family.

My mother was always the first to offer to make *sheva berachos*, whether it was for one of our *bachurim* or one of the girls for whom she had arranged a *shidduch*. Back then, it wasn't like nowadays. Now a *sheva berachos* is often a fancy expensive affair. Then, my mother would quickly put something on the stove from whatever was in the house. She took from here, she took from there, she quickly called in the *bachurim*, and suddenly, in a matter of moments, the house was full of *simchah* and singing. It was the *simchah* of the mitzvah that made it so beautiful.

In those days, the last bus out of Yerushalayim was at seven o'clock. Anyone who came for a wedding had to stay the night. Our beds were often needed for the guests. It was quite a sight to see guests sleeping on every available surface!

When we grew up, the five of us spent many nights sleeping in our parents' beds. We knew that we would go to sleep in our own beds but we never knew exactly where we would awaken in the morning.

Once at about two o'clock in the morning, the house was full of guests who had stayed after a wedding. Everyone was preparing to go to sleep when suddenly there was a knock on the door. When my mother opened it, who stood there but one of the Rabbis and his 16-year-old daughter. They had planned to sleep at another family's home but when they knocked at the door, no one answered. Where could they go at such an hour? To the home of Rav Chadash, of course! One of the *bachurim* gave the Rav his bed and I gave my trundle bed to his daughter. It was too short for me and my father had removed the wooden end, so that my feet stuck out. We had "solved the problem" by putting a chair at the end of the bed so my feet would have something to rest on. None of us minded giving up our bed to a guest. No one even questioned it. And to this very day, I can sleep in any bed, under any conditions, because that is how I grew up!

My mother was stubborn about her mitzvos. Once she became involved in a project, she saw it through to the end — no matter how hard the going got. Especially with matchmaking, her personal investment knew no bounds. She would become as intensely involved with the potential bride and groom as if he or she were her very own child.

One *shidduch* in particular took a seemingly endless amount of her time and energy. Way back then, there were no private phones. This meant that my mother traveled back and forth across town trying to arrange the *shidduch*. Transportation in Jerusalem in those days was time-consuming and costly, yet that didn't stop her from making her way from one end of the city to another in pursuit of an agreement from both sides.

In the end, *baruch Hashem,* the couple were wed. A few weeks before the wedding, the *chasan's* father came to visit. My mother was delighted, and sat him down at the table. "Rebbetzin," he began, as he took an envelope out of his pocket, "there is no way we can ever thank you for everything you have done, so at least please accept this."

She knew the envelope contained money, *shadchan gelt.* She just smiled at the father and said, "My happiness is to see the children happy."

But this time she had met her match, because the father wouldn't take "no" for an answer. Finally, my mother seemed ready to give in. "Okay," she said, "you can give the money. Just please excuse me for a moment."

She sent my brother out of the house to the neighbor who was the secretary of the *kollel.* Within 10 minutes this man came with his receipt book. She showed him to the table where the father was sitting. "Please sit down. I have a donation for you." Then she turned to the father and smiled, "Okay, I'll take the money but the Rabbi will write a receipt."

After the Six-Day War, the whole family took a taxi to Chevron to see where the yeshivah had been located and where they had lived. We went up the steps and entered the room. What was the first thing that my mother told me? She pointed to an old cracked and splintered window frame. By this window once, during *seudah shelishis* stood a *bachur* who became the Rav of Magdil, HaRav Mayani, *zt"l.* He looked out towards the twilight and at the new stars that were coming out. Very slowly he sang in Yiddish, "*Ribbono shel Olam,* isn't it enough suffering?" Over and over he sang it for a long time in such a melody that all the *bachurim* became still to listen to him. He had no idea they were all listening. He didn't feel, he didn't know, he was lost in the song, in the suffering, in the longing. This was the first thing she showed us in the house where they used to live. This is the window, this is where he stood and sang.

Whenever one of the Rabbis would come to us for Shabbos, he would sit with my father and sing. This is what filled the air of our home.

People thought we had a very nice apartment, but the truth is that my parents never changed the furniture. It was always old. My mother would make sure there was a clean pressed tablecloth and the dishes were always shining. Our beds were the old type, made of iron.

Then the sad day came when my mother passed away. People came during the *shivah* but they couldn't believe it was the same apartment. It had always been so full of life and singing and love that no one ever noticed the old furniture.

During the *shivah*, many people came. They looked for the cookies in the basket on the table, with the coffee, tea and sugar. They walked straight into the kitchen to see if the big copper samovar was still standing.

That was what people remembered most.

From the Depth of Gratitude

The story of Clara Hammer's chicken fund, "On Wings of Inspiration," appears on page 179. Here we learn about some of the factors that went into making Mrs. Hammer the giving person she is. As she puts it, "With everything I have seen and lived through, I feel not only part of the chosen nation but also individually chosen to do Hashem's mission of taking care of some of the people who are not as fortunate."

Mrs. Hammer was born in a small town in Russia. At the age of four, with the outbreak of World War I, she and her siblings were sent by her mother to stay with relatives. Clara was sent to live with her Bubbie and Zeide. She remembers her Zeide's warmth and his special kindness to her. As a child, Clara was a finicky eater. So her Zeide would take her on his lap and teach her a *niggun*, a chassidic melody that has remained with her to this day. As he chanted the *niggun*, he would feed her. But this arrangement, unfortunately, did not last. One Monday, market day for the gentile farmers, Clara went as usual with her Bubbie and Zeide to town to buy their weekly chickens, eggs, onions, potatoes and beets for borscht. The farmers would bring their wagons, five or six of them, filled with wares, and stand them in the center of town, right in front of the synagogue. At first they would be covered. When the villagers would arrive the farmers would uncover the wagons and sell their merchandise.

That Monday, Clara's Zeide went to *shul* to *daven*. She and her Bubbie waited nearby. When the men finally came out of the *shul*, the farmers uncovered the wagons. But instead of chickens, eggs, onions and potatoes, the wagons were filled with men who jumped out of the wagons wielding hatchets, hammers and sticks. They beat up the Jewish men, herded them back into the *shul*, and set it on fire. Then they ran away. By the time the fire was put out, Clara's Zeide and three other men were terribly burned. To the heartbreak of the family, her Zeide died.

But Zeide's *niggun*, the melody that flamed in her Zeide's heart, had kindled a spark in hers. She never forgot his melody and she never forgot the warmth of his kindness.

After the death of her Zeide, Clara returned home. A few years later there were pogroms in the town. Clara, her parents, and a younger brother and sister were making their escape when suddenly they were surrounded by the peasants who lived on the outskirts of the town. The leader was mounted on a horse, with a cruel look of glee on his face. But Clara's father recognized him. He ran up in front of him and said, "You're going to harm me and my family? Don't you remember working for us? Don't you remember how every day my mother would bring you tea and cake?"

The peasant stared towards the forest, speechless, for what seemed like hours. Then he commanded gruffly, "Follow me." He led them through the woods. When they reached a certain point, he turned to go back and said, "Now you are safe."

In 1997, Mrs. Hammer had the privilege of rejoicing at the *bris* of her 32nd great-grandchild. As she stood with the women she heard, "And his name will be called in Israel, Avraham Yonah." Her heart skipped a beat because that was the name of her Zeide!

After the *bris*, they brought little Avraham Yonah to his "Great Savta." She held him on her lap and hummed her Zeide's *niggun* to him. She said to the people around her, "He is the sixth generation, *bli ayin hara*. There was my grandfather, my father, I, my daughter, my grandson, and this is my great-grandson. And he is in Yerushalayim, the city about which my grandfather sang *'L'shanah Haba'ah b'Yerushalayim.' Baruch Hashem*, we are here."

These are a mere fraction of the motivating episodes that fuel Mrs. Hammer's drive to fill each moment with gratitude and mitzvos. As she movingly says, "This is it. When I remember what I lived through — the pogroms and the miracles, my imprisonment at the age of nine when I was sick with measles and had to beg for a piece of bread — and then I see my great-grandchildren, it gives me the strength and *emunah* to believe that Hashem saved me for a purpose. The best way I can express my gratitude is by filling my days with kindness for other people."

☙ *Almond Milk*

In our house there was no such thing as a jar of commercially prepared baby food. As far as my mother was concerned, it might as well have had a skull and crossbones printed on the label. When asked why, she would laugh. "Your Bubbie never took us to doctors. She went into her kitchen and produced herbal concoctions whose smell was enough to scare away any ailment!

"Although, as a child, I hated those bitter medicines, I was shocked into a new level of regard for her knowledge when I saw what happened with cousin Bernie."

And then, inevitably, as she skimmed every bit of fat from the chicken soup before it went into the blender with carrots and onions — her own pure baby food — my mother would tell the almond milk story once again. Here it is in her own descriptive words.

"When cousin Bernie, may he live and be well, was a little boy, he was so very sick that they had to put him in the hospital in Springfield. Something, they didn't know what, was terribly wrong with his stomach.

"One Shabbos, a messenger came to the house to tell Bubbie, may she rest in peace, that the doctors had given up and Bernie was dying. Now you know your Bubbie was a strictly religious woman. On Shabbos she was in another world. But on this particular Shabbos she got up from her books and went straight to the door. 'I'm going to speak to the Rav.' Moments later she was in the kitchen.

" 'Mama,' I asked her, 'what are you doing?'

" 'Saving a life,' she answered.

"She took almonds and put them in boiling water. Then, one by one, she peeled them. She crushed them fine, like sand, and mixed them with cool boiled water. Then she strained the whole mixture through a cheesecloth. I could not believe my mother was doing all this on Shabbos. As she worked she whispered something, but I couldn't hear what it was. When the mixture was ready, she put it in a jar and said to me, '*Kum*, Rochele.'

"I don't know what the doctors thought of this four-foot-eleven-inch, gray-haired Yiddish-speaking woman holding a jar in her hand, but they were so desperate that they agreed to let Bubbie give my cousin the almond milk.

"There was Bernie, lying in the hospital bed with his worried parents hovering close by. As soon as she entered, Bubbie walked over to her sister and said confidently, 'Don't worry, G-d will heal him.' She raised up the jar of beige-white almond milk, 'This will help.'

"But Bernie didn't want to drink it.

"I had just gotten my first wristwatch. It was such an event for me. I was all of 13, and in those days to have your own wristwatch meant you were very, very grown up. I don't know what possessed me at that moment, but I took off my treasured watch and said, 'Bernie, if you listen to my

Mama and drink a few drops, I promise I'll give you my new watch.'

"Everyone held their breath as Bernie took my watch in his thin fingers and Bubbie put the cup of almond milk to his lips.

"Well, you know G-d can do anything. And I'm telling you the truth, within the hour, the color came back to his face and he asked for mashed potatoes! The doctor said, 'Mrs. Davis, I don't know what was in that jar, but it healed him.'

"Your Bubbie looked that doctor straight in the eye and said in Yiddish, 'The *Ribbono shel Olam* hears prayers, and He heals us.'"

Modesty

❧ The Mantle of Royalty

Women are the bearers of the inner sanctity of Klal Yisrael. Knowing this lofty concept in our minds and embracing it in our hearts so that it becomes a deep part of who we are is one of our greatest challenges. Rebbetzin Miriam Mann, of blessed memory, was a person who embodied this awareness with her whole being. Even when faced with a life-threatening illness, the knowledge of who she truly was never left her. May Hashem help us to recognize that resting within the beauty of concealment is our royal soul, which bears the imprint of holiness for all generations to come.

Rebbetzin Miriam Mann was the daughter of Rav Vitkin, a *talmid* (student) of the Saba of Slobodka. She was the wife of Rav Mann, the *Rosh Yeshivah* of Yeshivah Beis Hillel in Bnei Brak. At the age of 54, Rebbetzin Mann was struck with a serious illness which put her at risk of cerebral hemorrhage. She was advised to travel immediately to America for brain surgery.

At that time, the routine procedures before surgery, checking blood pressure and other preparations, were done in one central ward. It was explained to the Rebbetzin that all patients scheduled for surgery that day, both men and women, were prepared in the same ward. The hospital staff reassured her that everyone was kept covered by a sheet and that the close friend who had accompanied her would be allowed to remain with her at all times.

When she heard all this, Rebbetzin Mann firmly stated, "I will not go in there."

The nurse was equally emphatic. "You must. Otherwise, we won't be able to treat you."

The Rebbetzin only repeated quietly, "I will not go in there."

The close friend accompanying her tried to convince the Rebbetzin not to make such a fuss about it. "Miriam, this is a matter of life and death. This is how things are done here in America. I'll be right next to you and I'll make sure to hold the sheet. You have to be properly prepared for the operation, otherwise they won't treat you."

Rebbetzin Mann remained standing outside the door to the preparation room. She looked at her friend and said, "I will not go in there."

The nurse standing nearby threw up her hands in exasperation and said to the Rebbetzin's friend, "Explain to her that this is standard hospital procedure. She is scheduled for major surgery in a few hours and we simply have no other place to put her. She came here all the way from Israel. Please do your best to convince her to be more reasonable."

Just then, Professor Merken, the surgeon who was to perform the operation, passed by on his way into the room. "Good morning, Rebbetzin Mann. What seems to be the problem?"

It was explained to the doctor that due to the Rebbetzin's standards of modesty and her insistence that to be in such a place, even if she were completely covered by a sheet, was a violation of Torah law, she adamantly refused to enter for the routine preparation.

Professor Merken motioned to the nurse. "Audrey," he said, "I've never before encountered such a person. Please calm yourself and leave her alone." He hesitated for a moment and then in a voice of resolve continued, "Prepare the

Presidential Suite. We are caring for a dignitary."

"The Presidential Suite! But Professor Merken — we have no official authorization."

"That's a detail, Audrey, that I will handle personally at another time."

Professor Merken strode down the hall to the two women who stood conversing quietly.

"Rebbetzin, you can rest assured that you will be taken care of in strict adherence to your faith. I have never before met anyone like you. We have a special emergency room in the hospital reserved for the President and other prominent dignitaries. I have given orders to my head nurse that it be opened for you. So if you would kindly take the elevator to the seventh floor and wait outside room 719, the head nurse will be there shortly. I'll come to check you within the hour."

The Rebbetzin stood there with her close friend. Far from her home and family, in a foreign country and a strange environment, she hoped and prayed that the medical professionals would be heavenly messengers to heal her. Faced with such a crisis, she could have easily been overtaken by fear and unfamiliarity. But she would allow neither environmental factors nor her personal circumstances to alter her stance. As she conducted herself in her home, so she acted in the hospital. Her inner connection with her Creator remained whole and perfect. She was able, in her quietly assertive way, to communicate her convictions to the authorities. When the mantle of royalty is worn with dignity and self-respect, it is recognized by Jew and non-Jew alike.

❧ No More Cover-ups

This Rebbetzin currently teaches in a well-known, highly respected girls seminary. Hearing the following story about her younger years, we find it easy to relate to her struggles. What a relief to realize that "great people are made, not born"!

When her parents died suddenly, it took Chayah quite a while to recover from the shock. She and her friend went to board with a family, and little by little she began to participate in all the regular activities of a teenager. Of this period in her life she has said, "I felt like every day was full of darkness. There were times when I was angry that the sun was shining and the sky was clear blue. How dare the sun shine when I am so broken. But, little by little, I began to put the pieces of my life back together."

She and her friend were often invited elsewhere on Shabbos. One day, Chayah's friend told her they were going to the home of a very warm chassidic Rebbetzin. The thought of going there made Chayah feel a little embarrassed because, at that time, she wore sleeves above her elbow. She knew this wasn't proper, so she put on a cardigan before walking over.

When she arrived, the Rebbe sat down at the table and asked her about her family. "Who was your grandfather?"

"Rabbi Adams."

"Rabbi Adams from Boston?"

"Yes," she answered in astonishment.

The Rabbi said, "That's amazing! He was a frequent visitor at our home. So you are Rabbi Adams' granddaughter. It's such a privilege to have you in our home."

Chayah responded with a warm smile. Inwardly, though, she was churning. It bothered her that she was there on what seemed to be false pretenses. She felt she was putting on an act, that she wasn't the nice *tzniusdik* girl they thought she was. Why, only a few hours before, she had been walking around in short sleeves!

Inside, something was gnawing away at her. She really admired the Rebbetzin. She had always felt the Rebbetzin was the most wonderful, genuine and sincere person she had ever met. This generous invitation to join her family on Friday night and Shabbos day, and the warmth exuded by the Rebbetzin in her home had cemented all those feelings. That's what made Chayah wonder, "How can I keep up a double standard in the face of such an authentic kind person? And how can I be a hypocrite to my grandfather?"

As she walked home with her friend, Chayah was unusually quiet. Her friend sensed that something was bothering her, but didn't ask any questions.

Chayah gave her sleeve length a lot of thought. "You have to make a choice," she told herself firmly. "You can't be a hypocrite. You can't walk into the Rebbetzin's home with long sleeves and then half an hour later wear short sleeves somewhere else." Personal integrity won out. And pride. "If she ever found out, you would be very, very embarrassed," she clinched the argument with herself.

Then and there she made what she likes to call her "choice for the better." She gave away all of her short-sleeved clothing, and from that moment on wore only clothes that covered her elbows.

When she looks back at that time in her life, she realizes what being in that Rebbetzin's home meant to her. "It was who she was — not what she said — that affected me in such a positive way," Chayah notes. "It was her genuine warmth and caring. Being in the atmosphere of her Shabbos table helped me realize that the choice of covering my elbows was well worth it. The Rebbetzin never said a *thing* to me about my clothes. She wanted to know about my family and my studies, and I was grateful that she was so interested in me. I don't know what I would have done if she had given me a lecture. Who knows where I would be today?"

~ *A New Friend*

> *Our Sages tell us that tochachah (reproof) must stem from care and concern for the other person. In this story, a spirited dynamic Rebbetzin demonstrates how rebuke appropriately given with a loving heart can have a ripple effect of lasting benefit. (This story originally appeared in the Yated Ne'eman.)*

It was Shabbos afternoon in Jerusalem, and Devorah was hurrying home from a *shiur* in time for *seudah shelishis*. She was wearing her good black wool Shabbos skirt ... which she knew had a slit that needed sewing up. She had tried to sew it by hand after she bought it, but somehow the stitches unraveled. The next time she wore it, she tried pinning the edges of the slit together, but the pins never managed to stay closed and in place. Being recently married and just setting up her new apartment, Devorah didn't yet own a full-length mirror. In all honesty, she really didn't know how the slit looked when she was wearing the skirt. Although she did feel a little uneasy wearing it, her wardrobe was limited since she hadn't yet unpacked all of her clothes. "Besides," she told herself, "so many other women are walking around with slits in their skirts." In short, it just wasn't her first priority.

Now, as she walked quickly, her thoughts were on getting home in time to set the table before her husband's return. Suddenly, from behind, she heard a very sweet, yet at the same time intense, voice. "Excuse me, sweetheart, do you mind if I speak with you for a minute?" She turned around and found herself face to face with Rebbetzin Chaya Heyman, the wife of the Rav of one of the neighborhood's most prominent *shuls*, and a highly respected teacher in Bais Yaakov.

"Shalom, Rebbetzin Heyman, good Shabbos. It's so nice to meet you in person — until now, I've only had the pleasure of speaking with you on the phone."

"Listen," the Rebbetzin began, with a slightly perceptible hesitation in her voice. Devorah felt her heart pound in nervousness as she wondered what the Rebbetzin was going to tell her. "I see," Rebbetzin Heyman continued gently, "that you are a person who is concerned with *tznius*. Your hair is covered very beautifully, your skirt length is fine, and you are walking in a very modest way."

Devorah relaxed a little upon hearing these compliments.

"Why, I'll bet that you really have no idea," the Rebbetzin smiled, "that every time you take a step, part of your upper leg is visible to the eye! You didn't know that, did you?"

Devorah took a deep breath and looked into Rebbetzin Heyman's eyes. It was a moment in time when Devorah would have liked nothing better than for the pavement to open up and drop her onto a totally different planet. This was the Rebbetzin she had been wanting to meet for such

Modesty / 143

a long time. This was the person about whom her best friend had said, "She doesn't usually give classes for the community. But if you ever have an opportunity to hear her speak, don't miss it. She is a rare and unusual human being."

Devorah felt the full force of the Rebbetzin's high voltage energy focused solely on her. She swallowed before offering an excuse. "You're right, Rebbetzin," she finally managed to squeak out. "But I really didn't know. I tried to close it with safety pins, but they popped out." The words sounded weak even to her own ears.

"That's all right, darling. Another time, when it's not Shabbos, you come over and I'll sew it up for you, one-two-three! By the way, when did you move into the neighborhood?"

The two women chatted for several minutes, and then Devorah dashed home, her mind still on the encounter. Along with the happiness she felt at having finally met the famous Rebbetzin were mingled feelings of embarrassment over the circumstances of their meeting. Upon further reflection, she realized that if anyone knew how to teach people about *tznius*, it was Rebbetzin Heyman! First of all, she herself was always beautifully dressed. Secondly, not for one minute had Devorah felt criticized, even though she had wanted to drop through the floor. She came away feeling praised! The Rebbetzin had seen her as a person concerned about *tznius* and had even complimented her. Most of all, Devorah said to herself, the Rebbetzin really cared about me. She didn't treat me like a stranger, but like a friend.

She decided to take the Rebbetzin up on her offer, and the following week, as they sewed up the slit, a friendship began that is still going strong many years later.

🖋 The Power of Praise

Rebbetzin Fried has been a teacher and educator for the past 30 years. Her care and concern for all Jewish daughters extends far beyond the walls of her classroom. The following story is an example of how the power of praise and kind words spoken from a sincerely caring heart can help people change for the better. Although at first glance this incident may not seem dramatic, the inner conviction to speak to the manager of a wedding hall about his staff is really an extraordinary act of courage.

Rebbetzin Fried approached the wedding hall with her heart filled with excitement, and gratitude, too. Her Sarah'le was getting married!

Sarah'le had lived with them ever since she was 14. Raised in the midwest, born to a Jewish mother who intermarried, she had somehow found her way to the Rebbetzin. The first few years were fraught with battles. The angry threatening phone calls from Sarah's parents came weekly.

"What we went through," she reflected now. And then the fight to get Sarah'le into a good school! That had really been something. Now, *baruch Hashem,* 10 years later, peace was restored to the family. She hoped the wedding would get Sarah's new life off to a good fresh start.

After the *chupah*, the photographer gathered the families of the *chasan* and *kallah* outside to take dozens of pictures. When Rebbetzin Fried finally entered the wedding hall, she was happy to see that so many members of the community had come to participate. She had been on the phone for hours the week before reminding her friends about the invitation and pleading with them to make room in their busy schedules to attend.

But as she approached the women's side of the buffet, her heart sank. What greeted her eyes spoiled the whole wedding.

It was the waitresses. They were lovely young girls — but the way they were dressed! She was so hurt and upset, she was beside herself. The irony struck her: The hall was filled with prominent Rabbis and Torah scholars (the result of her many phone calls) being served by waitresses whose attire did not meet the standards of modesty to which the guests were accustomed.

While she was standing there debating what to do, her two best friends walked in. She was sure they would share her feelings. She walked over to them and said, "Do you see what I see?"

They nodded.

"This place is under new management, and the caterer is just starting out. I'm sure he's under a lot of pressure and doesn't even notice how these waitresses are dressed."

"You're probably right," her friends answered.

"So come with me and we'll all go together to the office and ask the manager nicely if he can do something about it."

"Oh, I couldn't do that. I'm just not the type," one friend answered.

"It's a good idea, but I wouldn't know what to say," said the other.

Alone — but determined — the Rebbetzin went to find the manager's office. If she had to, she'd do it herself. Human nature, she mused, is to refrain from saying something because you are afraid. We think: How will they look at me? How will they receive me? What if they yell at me? What if they embarrass me?

She, too, worried about the manager's reaction. But inside, she was cringing from embarrassment because of those outfits. No matter how the manager reacts, she told herself, things could not get worse, they could only get better. And it was up to her, because if she didn't take the initiative, no one else was going to. "If I am not for myself, who will be for me?" she thought, to give herself courage.

At that point, she found the office. Before she went in, she said a quick prayer. "Please, Hashem, put the right words in my mouth. Please help me to speak kindly and softly and to do this for Your honor, not for myself."

The Rebbetzin looked into the manager's office and saw three men sitting there. They appeared tired and concerned. Taking a deep breath, she walked in with a big smile on her face and said, "I came to compliment you on your beautiful wedding hall. It is really elegant. The meal looks so splendid and delicious and the people are enjoying it so much."

She herself hadn't eaten a thing, but those who were eating looked like they were enjoying the food and even commented that it was good, so she wasn't lying. The three men stood up and smiled. The Rebbetzin was encouraged by their warm response. She knew how much work went into catering, a business fraught with tremendous pressure. She also knew that complaints were handed out more liberally than compliments, and that praise was music to a caterer's ears.

"You must have worked very hard to get this affair to run so smoothly and beautifully," she continued. "But," she searched carefully for the right words, "one thing hurts me very much. I see that the waitresses you hired are dressed in such an unbecoming way. It just doesn't fit in with the rest of the atmosphere. You have a place that's so elegant, a place that caters to the religious population — it's embarrassing to have girls dressed like that serving food to the men. It's not in accordance with Jewish law. Your establishment is glatt kosher, so your staff should dress in a respectful way because, you know, they represent you to the public."

The manager digested those comments before saying to the Rebbetzin, "You are 100 percent right. All I can say in my defense is that I never thought of it. I hire the waitresses from an agency, and until this moment, I've just taken whatever outfits they send. But I guarantee you that this is going to change and I thank you for bringing it to my attention."

The manager walked out of the office and went to the kitchen to speak with the head waiter. The Rebbetzin overheard the conversation. It was very short. "This is a glatt kosher establishment and I want glatt kosher outfits for my staff."

The Rebbetzin was happily shocked. When the manager came out of the kitchen she said, "Thank you so much. May you have success in all you do. May you always be healthy and make *simchahs* for *Klal Yisrael*."

Two months later the Rebbetzin was visiting one of her friends who had been at the wedding. "I have good news for you," said the friend. "I went to a wedding last week at the same hall and thanks to you, the waitresses were dressed modestly and very beautifully. They looked really elegant."

"That's wonderful news. Did you go in and thank the management?"

"No, I didn't."

"We should never be ashamed to do what's right for G–d and His Torah," the Rebbetzin answered her friend, "and we must force ourselves, even if we are shy, to praise people when they make changes to do the right thing. Look at how far praise can go! I'm going to look up that number and call the manager right now!"

And that's exactly what she did.

⚜ In a Foreign Palace

While others were dreaming of romance and fame, all she wanted was a Jewish home, to live quietly, without fanfare, happy to be the backdrop to a simple man with simple children who kept the mitzvos and feared Hashem.

Bearing greatness within the confines of her orphaned world, she kept her dreams to herself and grew into a woman. How Hashem, Maker of beauty and charm, created her destiny, the destiny of her nation! As they dragged her, sad and depressed, to the palace of an evil man who crowned her, married her, and called her his queen, something she normally had to die for now revealed itself as the purpose of her life.

As she sat surrounded by the idols of the palace waiting for the moment to reveal her heritage, she waited as only a woman waits, saying, "Fast for me, pray for me, open your hearts." She fell on her face with ashes in her hair, drawn curtains darkening her royal chamber. "L-rd of the universe, I do not have anyone other than You. Forgive our sins and listen in our time of trouble" (*Me'am Lo'ez, Megillas Esther* 5:1). Over and over she whispered and lifted her eyes through history, casting her *tefillos* deeply into the final dawn.

Esther personified the character trait of modesty. Yet her life circumstances were diametrically opposite to her innermost being. She, who longed to be a hidden being, was forced to go out, in the public eye, in a foreign palace, surrounded by repugnant luxury and extravagance. Yet through it all, Esther retained her dignity and modesty. The true royal bearing of a Jewish daughter did not for one moment allow the murky forces of the world, the influences of wealth, or the intrigue of politics, to affect her. Instead, she, the one who remained pure and reserved, was a conduit for *kedushah* and influenced the world to such an extent that the salvation of the Jewish people came through her.

As it was with Esther, so must it be with us. To the extent that circumstances compel us to go out, we must carry the nobility of our seclusion with us, not allowing foreign influences to affect us. As the Temple's windows reflected light outward, as Esther remained unchanged by her circumstances, so must we go about our daily lives as beacons of sanctity. The future of *Klal Yisrael* rests on our ability to be like Esther — an inner being in a foreign palace.

Nature's Bounty

☙ The Cricket's Wisdom

How often during the course of an ordinary day are precious moments waiting for us — if we only look. Here, a busy young mother of five shares an important lesson she learned in front of the insect case at the Jerusalem Zoo.

This summer, Chanie Dolman and her husband took the children to the Jerusalem Zoo for the first time. They were surprised to discover this lush green oasis only a short drive away, at the outskirts of the city. When they walked in, they were greeted by a cooling breeze which came from the natural flowing springs and the hills which frame the valley.

The monkeys' antics on their private island right inside the main entrance delighted the whole family. They decided to let the children lead the way as they explored the rest of the zoo.

When they reached the entrance to the small animal house, Chanie hesitated, reluctant to leave the cool fresh air and enter the dark realm of boa constrictors and muskrats. But the incessant pleading of six-year-old Yossie conquered her resistance, and they went in.

When they got to the small insect case she was about to walk past it. She really had no desire to get a close look at things which sometimes scare her even in her own home, like spiders and giant ants. But she felt the tug of a small hand on her left elbow. "*Ima*, look at the cricket — he's eating!"

There on a dried twig was a cricket, holding a green blade of grass with one of his leg-arms, his overly large, protruding eyes acutely visible as Chanie stood separated by only a window pane. She had never had the privilege of watching a cricket eat. Now they all watched as he slowly and deliberately took millimeter-sized bites, one at a time, out of the freshly picked blade of grass, carefully making his way down the edge. She looked at the angular technology of his cricket body and then at the wide-eyed wonder of her son with his nose pressed up against the glass.

"*Ima*, he's eating!" he repeated, and Chanie, humbled somehow by her desire to rush past this display of G-d's handiwork, whispered into his ear, " '*Pose'ach es yadecha u'masbia l'chol chai ratzon …*' Hashem gives all living things exactly what they need. He made sure that this particular cricket right here has this blade of grass to eat."

And so she learned the lesson of the cricket: We can learn something from everything. Let's not rush by the present moment because the life's lesson contained within it is most precious.

The Donkey's Tzedakah

I met Mrs. Singer at a burnout-prevention conference for religious women in the helping professions. A therapist who specializes in the problems of survivors and their families, Mrs. Singer lectures extensively on the topics of nurturing families and creating hope for the future. Herself a survivor of the War, she told me that one of the things she clung to was a saying often repeated by her mother: "Remember, troubles come by themselves; simchahs you have to make." What is the source of Mrs. Singer's exceptional nurturing ability? The following story can give us some insight.

"In my home," Mrs. Singer reminisces, "one of the things we learned early on was care and respect for animals. Although we lived in the city of Amsterdam, nature was a very important part of our lives. We had a tiny garden which received daily attention and usually once a week my mother would announce, 'Today we picnic at the zoo.'

"My childhood was filled with moments of enchantment. Can you imagine the thrill of a five-year-old child being allowed to hold a bottle and feed a baby panther? Or picture the delight on my face when my father blew his special whistle and a hyena came running up to him?

"Children find it easy to relate to the world of animals and nature with an open and giving heart. Seeds of *chesed* and gentleness can be planted, for example, when a child is taught to stroke the fur of a tiny kitten. This can provide a foundation that can then be carried over to caring for people.

"In our house in Holland, which did not have central heating," continues Mrs. Singer, "the pussycat also got a hot-water bottle in her basket at night. This wasn't considered anything extraordinary — it was just the proper thing to do. I suppose that's why I was able to bring home the donkey. But let me start at the beginning of the story.

"I was married with five children. My youngest was two and we were living in a villa in a newly-built development on the outskirts of Jerusalem. Since then, *baruch Hashem*, so many new neighborhoods have come up that we are no longer on the outskirts. But at that time it was very much like living out in the country.

"One day, as I was coming home from the park with my youngest child, I saw something I simply couldn't believe. There was a donkey in the middle of the street, braying and crying. A crowd of children were standing around pointing and laughing. Some of the older boys were beating the donkey with a long wooden pole.

"I was outraged. This is not what our Torah teaches us about animals. I parked the baby's stroller on the sidewalk and walked right into that group of children, took the donkey by the reins, and led him away to safety. I don't know what possessed me but I turned to the children and said, 'I invite you all to my house for *seudah shelishis* this Shabbos,' and I pointed to my house. 'It's the one with the big garden. You can bring your friends and we will learn about the mitzvah of kindness to animals.'

"It must have looked very funny to see a woman walking down the street pushing a stroller with one hand and leading a donkey with the other, but I didn't care. I brought the donkey into our garden, gave him some fresh water in a bucket, gently washed his bruises, and put a cotton sheet over them. As I spoke to the donkey in low soothing tones I actually felt anguish over the way the children had tormented him. I began remembering long-forgotten details of my own childhood in Holland and realized how my life had been enriched from learning about animals."

As a teenager, Mrs. Singer had become a volunteer at the zoo. Now, as an adult, she appreciated how much she had learned about people and psychology just by understanding animals. She observed that some animals thrive on human contact and even get depressed without it. Others, like cats, are very independent, yet can act cool and reserved after a separation from their master. If this is the sensitivity of a cat, how careful we must be with people! Our Sages tell us we can learn modesty from a cat, diligence from ants, and loyalty from doves. In *Tanach*, we find frequent references to positive traits that can be learned from each animal. Yissachar, for instance, is compared to a donkey, because just as a donkey works constantly carrying heavy loads, so too, the Torah scholar is constantly learning.

"As I finished brushing the donkey," Mrs. Singer continues her story, "my 15-year-old son came home and was flabbergasted to discover that we now had a donkey as a pet (temporarily, we hoped)! We put up signs all around the neighborhood and notified surrounding areas, but in the meantime, the donkey recuperated in the shade of our fruit trees as my children fed him pails of carrots generously supplied by the fruit-and-vegetable man.

"As we grew more and more attached to the donkey, our neighbors discovered that they now had a 4 a.m. braying alarm clock. One by one, the complaints came in. We were quick to let people know that as soon as we could, we would find a place for the donkey to board.

"The first boarding place was a good four miles away, but that didn't stop our donkey from running back to us from the stable three times! Finally, we located a private family with a barn half a mile away, and this was more acceptable. Requests to use the donkey for fund-raising started coming in from various organizations. My children arranged for donkey rides to be given, with all the money going to *tzedakah*.

"The best thing was that the children began to learn more about caring for and respecting animals. And, by the way, that first Shabbos 10 children came for *seudah shelishis*. We learned together how Hashem gave us a special mitzvah, *peter chamor,* the redemption of the firstborn donkey. Why? Because the donkeys helped the Israelites carry their wealth out of Egypt. Can you imagine! This teaches us that when even the lowliest creature does good, it is not forgotten by Hashem."

~ The Life and Times of Mr. Pokey

We live in an age of over-stimulation. The media, no matter how diligently we try to restrict its entry to our homes, bombards us from all sides. Whether it's cellular phones or modems, musak in stores, airport announcements booming repetitively, we are constantly called upon to transport the inner sanctity of our homes with us into an alien world.

But from what is that sanctity built? Is it created only from those extra-ordinary moments of the fantastic, those times of personal miracle when Hashem lifts His veil of concealment and allows us a glimpse at the hidden workings in His scheme?

What of the "ordinary" moments in our daily lives? These are the plentiful building blocks of the character of the Jewish child, who is destined to carry our sacred Torah into future generations.

Yet how is he, with his child's vision of life, to know his Creator? Only with the help of his parents, who take these moments of "ordinary existence" and infuse them with a recognition of the Divine.

The uniqueness of this story lies in its very ordi-

nariness. We have the choice to let each moment go by unrecognized, or to take that moment and highlight its special message — which is exactly what Mrs. Bodkin in the following story did.

Mr. Pokey, a millimeter-sized pale gray incandescent guppy, was born at six o'clock on a Wednesday in the middle of winter.

"Mommy," Mrs. Bodkin heard an excited whisper, "the fish is having babies." Mrs. Bodkin had been luxuriating in the extra five minutes of wake-up time allowed her by the snooze alarm. With two minutes left to go, she reluctantly opened her eyes. The face of her 11-year-old daughter, Menuchah, greeted her. "Mommy," she repeated urgently, "come watch with me."

Mrs. Bodkin made a mental calculation of how long this disruption of the morning routine might take and calculated the consequences. She'd have to drive three of her six children to school. The schools were not near each other and it might set her back an hour. Was it worth giving up an hour of her morning to share this miracle of Hashem's handiwork with her children?

Yes, she decided, most emphatically; the answer could only be yes.

Within five minutes, she, Menuchah and now Aryeh were gathered around the fish tank. They could hear the constant soothing purr of the air filter as the bubbles rose to the surface of the water lit by a fluorescent lamp. The mother fish was suspended in her special isolation tank that had a slotted plastic grid for the speck-like baby guppies to slide through. This was a safety measure for the newborns whose mother might otherwise eat them. The mother fish swam around, then darted a bit more jaggedly from side to side and then suddenly, out popped a baby guppy which immediately fell down through the grid to the lower level of the isolation tank. Mother fish repeated her performance at least 35 times within the next half hour, much to the amazement of the now eight wide-eyed spectators.

As the children awoke one by one, they stationed themselves in awestruck silence around the illuminated glass fish tank. And when Mr. Bodkin stepped through the door with his usual cheery, "Good morning, sweeties," he was greeted by a cheering section of pajama-clad children all talking at once.

"What's going on here?" he asked, both confused and concerned. "I hope no one is sick."

"No, Daddy, *baruch Hashem*," Aryeh spoke up. "It's just that the guppy is having babies. We think she's almost finished. Come see."

All the children grabbed hold of their amused father, latching on to whatever part they could manage to reach, and pulled him toward the tank. Two-year-old Yoni grabbed his Daddy's knee. "See, fishie babies," he said, summing up the situation rather succinctly.

With a look of resignation mingled with genuine curiosity, Mr. Bodkin allowed himself to be pulled over to the tank. Soon he, too, was staring in fascination. Finally, the amazing performance was finished. Menuchah took the net, gently picked up the mother fish, and let her back down into the regular tank.

"You'll get a lot more exercise in there," she whispered. She picked up the slotted portion that separated the babies from the hungry mother like a protective fence. Devorah ran to the drawer where they kept the finely powdered baby fish food.

"Remember," said Mrs. Bodkin, "not too much." The

whole family watched as the babies took their first bites.

"Okay, kids, time to get dressed quickly," Mrs. Bodkin broke the quiet. "I'll drive whoever needs to be driven, and for those of you who might be a little late, I'll write a special 'fish note'!"

Over breakfast the family discussed the *berachah* "*HaMalach HaGoel*" and how privileged they had been to see a real-life example of "to multiply like fish in the midst of the earth."

"But still," insisted Menuchah, " how could it be in the middle of dry land?"

"Excellent question," said her father. "Please ask me that again later today — after you've spent at least some time in school."

Mrs. Bodkin made sure she had everyone in the station wagon and off they went with a surprisingly low margin of lateness. As she drove home with little Yoni he kept up a constant chant: "Fishie babies, fishie babies." Mrs. Bodkin contemplated her decision that morning. What if Menuchah had been a boy? Would I have let him stay to watch and arrive late? Probably not. Aryeh started school at eight-thirty and his class didn't begin to *daven* until ten to nine, so he hadn't even been late.

She decided to defrost her reserve casserole of baked macaroni for dinner, to make up the hour. That way, the rest of her schedule could stay pretty much routine.

Within a few days, the children's initial excitement had leveled off and the baby guppies were no longer the main topic of conversation in the house.

Until they started dying.

The little fish would be found one after the other floating on top of the birth tank's water. Finally, Mrs. Bodkin called the pet store.

"I don't understand what's happening," she said. "They were all healthy fish!"

"Turn off the light," the store owner suggested. "It's probably too hot and the algae are multiplying too quickly."

His advice helped somewhat, but by then they had already lost about half the batch, and over the next two months, all the baby guppies died except for one. They named this sturdy and curious fish, who seemed to explore every corner of his little incubation tank, Mr. Pokey. When the time came for Mr. Pokey to join the other fish in the big tank, he had no problem. He took to the big tank "like a fish takes to water," with none of the more senior residents bothering him.

Pesach cleaning in the Bodkin household began with a fresh coat of paint for the living room. To protect the fish tank from an accidental fall, Mrs. Bodkin placed it on the floor. But much to everyone's dismay, the workers moving one of the cabinets failed to see it, and, as they inched the heavy cabinet along the carpet, the sound of crashing glass was suddenly heard.

"Oh, no," cried Menuchah, who was the first to see what happened. "The fish tank!"

Sure enough, there was water spilling out all over the green rug and two fish were lying there on the floor. It was a moment that required quick thinking, and Mrs. Bodkin rose to the challenge. She ran to the kitchen for an old clear plastic salad bowl, filled it with water, and ran for the fish net.

"Look!" shouted Aryeh, "Mr. Pokey is okay. He's still swimming around in there as if nothing happened!" Mrs. Bodkin paused to admire the fish. His whole environment had just suffered the equivalent of an earthquake, yet there he was calmly darting to and fro. She caught him in the net and transferred him to the salad bowl, pouring in some of the water that was still left in the tank.

"Here's your new home, dearie," she said to him and placed the bowl on the bookshelf. "*Baruch Hashem*, at least we still have Mr. Pokey."

The other fish got an honorable farewell down the bathroom sink, while Mr. Pokey seemed to enjoy his spacious no-frills salad bowl on the bookcase.

The following week, the time came to clean Mr. Pokey's salad bowl in honor of Pesach. Menuchah and Aryeh were in charge. They placed the fish in a plastic cup filled with water and took the salad bowl to scrub and refill. Suddenly Aryeh cried out, "Menuchah, come quickly — he jumped out of the cup!"

"Oh no," Menuchah said sadly, certain that this time Mr. Pokey was gone forever.

"There he is!" exclaimed Aryeh. There on the floor, gasping for water, lay Mr. Pokey. Menuchah knew that it was no time to be squeamish. She quickly picked up Mr. Pokey and put him in the cup. "Here, Aryeh, please keep your hand on the cup and I'll get the bowl filled." Soon Mr. Pokey was restored to his bowl on the kosher-for-Pesach bookshelf, apparently having sustained no visible injury.

At dinnertime, as the family sat down to eat together, Menuchah and Aryeh told everyone what had happened.

"*Baruch Hashem*," their father said. "If he had jumped out on Shabbos it wouldn't have been so simple to just plop him back into the tank. Look at all the *chesed* Hashem has done for Mr. Pokey. He let him survive the overgrowth of algae, he lived through the destruction of the fish tank, he's living in a plain bowl without a fancy air filter, and now he just survived an accident without even a little scratch. If Hashem does all this for Mr. Pokey, think of how much He does for us and all the Jewish people, every second of every day."

Mr. Pokey graced the Bodkin household for over a year and a half, happily darting to and fro in his no-frills fish bowl on the bookcase. All this had a permanent impact on the Bodkin children. They were taught of the kindness Hashem does for his tiniest creatures; and were also shown a triumphant testimony to the tenaciousness of life.

"Mommy, How Could You Speak to the Rabbi About Cats?"

For a gadol, nothing in G-d's world is too minuscule or insignificant. As we see time and time again, true greatness is found in attention to small details. The fact that this internationally known posek took the time to listen to a shaylah about baby kittens is in and of itself a tribute to the importance of even the small wonders of creation.

"People think I love cats," begins Mrs. Trauber, "but that's not the point. Let me explain.

"I grew up with a deep appreciation for all living creatures. I was raised not to hurt a thing. Any beetle in our house — even a bumblebee, if possible! — was caught and set free. My father told me about the pussycats in the *shtetl* where he grew up, how they were a natural part of life there and how everyone would feed them. He was a Rabbi and a businessman, always doing *chesed,* but when he would call home he would invariably ask if the animals had been fed.

"Now I'm living in a modern apartment, not a *shtetl,* but we do have a garden, and the neighborhood cats come and we feed them. It's wonderful to watch them. Oh, it's a wonder to watch how a mother cat will guard her kittens when they're newborn but then gradually, when they get older, start taking them out for walks and teach them how to manage on their own. One particular mother cat is very special. A few months ago someone dropped a tiny kitten in here and this mother cat adopted the strange kitten and nursed her like her own. Animals don't usually do that, but this one did.

"Just the other day a neighbor's child came here with two newborn kittens. I told her, 'Bring those right back where you found them,' and I then explained why. I had a feeling that the mother cat was still there and these were so tiny that if they stayed with me they would have died. Later that day I felt I had to check up on those kittens. I finally found them up at the very top of the building in a little corner hidden away on a bed of rags. The mother cat must have known she needed a place far away from curious children. Don't you think I had to check up on those cats for a few days? I would think of them at night before I went to sleep, and prayed that Hashem was taking care of them.

"There should be more appreciation of the benefit cats bring. They still keep rodents and other pests away. I think it's only decent for people to put out water, especially in the summertime when its hot and dry.

"Once, many years ago, a mother cat had her kittens in our backyard. I was under a lot of stress at that time and watching the mother cat take care of her kittens relaxed me. Well, my kids gave me a hard time, saying, 'Mommy, it's too much for you right now, making sure the cats are okay.'

"I wondered if they were right. Maybe I was making too much of them.

"I decided to go to a well-known Rav, and ask him about the cats. Do you know what he told me? With a twinkle in his eye and his characteristic warmth, he said, 'You go right ahead and take care of those cats.'

"When I told my son in yeshivah that I had asked the Rav about cats he couldn't believe it. 'Mommy, how could you speak to the Rabbi about cats?!'

"But you see, the greater a person is, the more down to earth he is. The Rav knew exactly how I felt.

"I try to teach the neighborhood children to be kind to animals. They love to come into our garden and see all the trees and plants. I teach them that they should act naturally with animals, to just let them be and not scare them. I tell them that with animals it's 'live and let live,' and that they should never abuse them. This is the attitude that surrounded me in my childhood home and this is what I try to pass on to the children. Everything *HaKadosh Baruch Hu* makes in His world has a purpose and a place. We have a mitzvah to take care of His world. So I encourage people, 'Leave out water, be a mentch — Hashem put them here for a reason.'"

Kindness

🌿 Your Bubbie's Tzedakah

Although I never knew her, my own Bubbie was always an active presence in my life. I missed out on her challah and cholent, but I received something that impacts on my very being to this day. I grew up on her stories.

Fayge Chaya Davis immigrated from Minsk to Springfield, Massachusetts in the early 1900s. The daughter of a scholar and well-educated in her own right, I do not think she ever obtained tax-deductible status for her charitable activities. Nevertheless, her home was a 24-hour-a-day association for the needy. Whether it was sewing shrouds for the burial society, checking cherries for her basement barrel of "stomachache brandy," or arranging documents for a sudden "relative" who was seeking entry to the United States, anyone who walked through the door was sure to be taken care of.

As soon as I was old enough to sit still for more than two minutes, my mother, Rochel Kempner, started telling me stories of her childhood. These stories would surface mostly during moments of an ordinary day. We would be in the kitchen together or sewing hems at the dining-room table. When relatives would visit it was also prime time for stories. But never did she sit me down and say, "Okay, now I'm giving over family history." It was a natural process, something I absorbed through osmosis. Years later, looking back, I realize the preciousness of this inheritance. The following is one of the first stories I ever heard.

It was midnight and the Bronx apartment was quiet. They were sitting at the dining-room table, sewing. Buttons and scraps of fabric formed piles on the tabletop. Midnight, the time when most of the world is wrapped in sleep and the daily scrambling of existence has stopped, is always a good time for conversation. The atmosphere allows a mother to talk openly to her daughter, to allow for priorities to surface, for the depths of the heart to open.

Threading her needle with a double thread and knotting it beneath the new button, Mrs. Kempner began:

"You know, your Bubbie, may she rest in peace, was always busy with so many projects. One thing especially made a deep impression on me as a child and that was when she collected *tzedakah* for a Rabbi in Israel.

"Rabbi Perlman, G-d rest his soul, had a yeshivah in Teveryah. I remember he once came to our house. It happened to be the day that President Franklin Roosevelt died. Rabbi Perlman was a tall man with a gray beard. He always wore a long coat and a black felt hat, a gentleman to the core. I remember how he was sitting in the living room that day when we heard the news on the radio. We started to cry.

" 'Why are you crying?' the Rabbi asked us in Yiddish. 'G-d is not dead! The world still stands!' That's the kind of person he was.

"And I want you to know," my mother looked up from her sewing to stress the importance of what she was about to say, "that people came from all over the city to give your Bubbie *tzedakah* for Rabbi Perlman. It's hard nowadays to understand how difficult the times were then, how important it was to help. Bubbie was always sending food, money, and whatever might be needed, sometimes even things like coats and pillows, depending on the postal service and what it would accept.

"I'll never forget one day in particular. World War II was raging in Europe, and America had entered the war. Bubbie gathered all the young men in the neighborhood who had been drafted and were leaving to go overseas and told each one, 'Give me a dollar for charity before you go. I will send your name to Rabbi Perlman in *Eretz Yisrael* for a blessing that G-d keep special watch over you so that you come home safely.'

"Sweetheart, I get the chills when I remember this, because there was one boy who laughed at my mother. 'Oh, Mrs. Davis,' he said with a mocking expression on his face, 'I don't believe in all that stuff. Do you really think that dollar will keep me safe?'

"My mother gently tried to coax him into giving the money. But the more she tried, the more stubborn he became in his refusal.

"I want you to know," she peered at me intently over her glasses, "that every single boy who gave that dollar for charity came back from the war healthy, whole and complete. The boy who laughed also came back. But he had lost one arm."

My mother wrapped the thread around the button and knotted the last knot on the underside.

"Mamma'le, you grew up in an entirely different world. We don't realize how much we have. But you should always know — and remember — that this is who your Bubbie was."

✒ He Who Resuscitates the Dead

Mrs. Davis was no stranger to life's hardships. Her first three children were stillborn, and although the doctor in "the old country" told her she would never have any others, she went on to raise a family of seven!

She was a woman of deep faith, in whom family, friends and neighbors found a warm heart and listening ear for their troubles. Often they would ask her if they should travel to a famous Rabbi or sage for a blessing. Then she would say to them in her special Yiddish-accented English, "Mamma'le, you want a bruchah? Go and help someone and the Aibishter will bentch you!" Then she would proceed to tell the story of how her daughter Rochel was born, vivid testimony to the soundness of her advice.

Home births were common in the early 1900s. In New England, some homes were built with special birthing rooms right off the kitchen. The Davis' house didn't have a birthing room, but Mrs. Davis always prepared the living room for that purpose. Their family doctor, Dr. Pine, was quite devoted to the family. He would come and settle himself in the worn gray armchair, while Zeide said *Tehillim*, ready to wake Dr. Pine when needed. Mrs. Davis' sisters usually came to keep the other children out of the living room.

Dr. Pine slept through most of this particular birth, Mrs. Davis' last, because at the time she had a close friend from Europe living with them who just happened to be a midwife. Sadie Berkowitz was a widow who had arrived in America a few years earlier. She had planned to live with her children but, for a reason never mentioned, it hadn't worked out. Well, that was all Mrs. Davis needed to hear. She moved her oldest daughter Chani in with the three youngest ones and announced that "Bubbie Sadie" was coming to live with the family. Everyone wanted to know how they were getting another Bubbie. Mrs. Davis would answer, "When G-d sends a blessing, we don't ask questions." Little did she know the prophetic spirit in her words, because it turned out that Bubbie Sadie saved her baby.

Bubbie Sadie looked like the description of a witch. She wore men's shoes, heavy stockings, and blouses with puffed sleeves and a tailored neckline; her dirndl skirts reached her ankles. Over all this she wore a long white pinafore held together by two safety pins. She had snowy white hair that she wore in a bun, and hardly any teeth. In fact, in the front, except for two almost fang-like eyeteeth, she was toothless. If a child didn't know her, he would be frightened. But up close, she had such special eyes. They were deep blue, an almost purple-blue. Her skin was milky white with just a blush of pink. She must have been a beautiful woman in her day.

While Dr. Pine slept, Bubbie Sadie attended the delivery. Mr. Davis must have been a little nervous at the thought of only a midwife helping his wife, so towards the end, he woke Dr. Pine.

The story goes that the baby didn't cry when she was born and that Dr. Pine took one look and told Mrs. Davis, "I'm so sorry, but this baby is not living."

He turned her upside down and shook her, but nothing happened. That's when Bubbie Sadie grabbed the limp baby from the doctor's hands and screamed, "No! This baby is not dead. This baby is very much alive."

As Bubbie Sadie used to say when she told the story, it all happened very fast. First she put the baby in cold water and then in water that was a little warmer than normal. Back and forth, back and forth, she kept immersing her in the water. And all of a sudden, the baby let out a little cry.

Bubbie Sadie held the infant in her arms even after they knew she was going to be okay. She used to say that she held her and held her and held her until the baby had a feeling of security.

When Mrs. Davis told this story she would say, "Oy, what would have happened, G-d forbid, if I hadn't taken her in!"

The "baby" in the tale would always end the story thoughtfully, "Maybe, that's why my nature is the way it is. Maybe I have so much love to give because I was loved immediately. And this lady we called Bubbie Sadie gave me that at birth. So now you see," she would tell her daughter, "the truth in your Bubbie's words, 'Go help someone and the *Aibishter* will *bentch* you.' She didn't learn it from a book — she lived it in her life."

Not for Reward

During the course of writing this book, this story from her childhood was "rediscovered" by my mother, Mrs. Rochel Kempner. She dug into the recesses of her memory to find this overlooked treasure. She is the Rochele in the story.

It was Saturday night on 49 Allendale Street. The children and their friends were standing in the living room near the piano deciding what to play and sing. The kitchen had become the women's section while Papa Davis sat with friends in the dining room. Five-year-old Rochele, the youngest child, was searching for the most interesting spot in the house. She was undecided between listening to the music or to the adult conversation when suddenly she heard a slightly raised voice come from the dining room.

"Shimon, we are like brothers, right? Tell me, how can you let all these people take such advantage of you? You have a big house with two extra apartments. It's the depression. You need the rent money. A person has to be kind, but please, business is business. You also have to live."

Rochele hid herself behind the door frame and peeked in to look at her father. He seemed tired. He was holding his mouth like he did when her brothers got into a lot of mischief. She saw him turn to his friend and say softly, "How can I have a roof over my head while my people are out in the cold? They are poverty stricken. If G-d wants me to have more money, He can give it to me. But right now what He wants me to do is to give these people a home."

Rochele was the youngest of seven, but she never felt poor. Even though she knew that her dresses were made-over hand-me-downs, and her shoes were patched and repatched many times, "poor" was a word that just didn't describe her home. Her life was a happy one. They grew vegetables in the backyard garden, and her kitten, Tiger Pussycat, lived in the garage. She loved the baked potatoes that she carried to school in the wintertime. They kept her hands warm and made a delicious lunch. The house was always filled with people and music.

Rochele never knew when she would wake up in her sister's bed covered by the big black woolen overcoat, which meant that a midnight guest had come to their home in need of a bed. No, she decided, they weren't rich, but they definitely weren't poor.

Her mother and father would always tell her that one mitzvah brings another. "When you do a mitzvah, it's the beginning of creating a miracle," they'd say. "We all have to look to do three extra mitzvos every day. There are seven days in a week, so by Shabbos, you will have done 21 extra mitzvos. If you multiply that by 52 weeks in a year, you have 1,092 extra mitzvos!

"We never know if a mitzvah is big or small. To the person who needs just a drink of water and cannot get it for himself, giving him a drink is a big mitzvah. You must always remember that G-d put you there in that place at that time to do that particular mitzvah. We never know what miracles come about as a result."

The next morning Rochele overheard her parents talking.

"The rent money is late, Fayge," her father was saying, "but don't say anything about it to Mr. and Mrs. Goldman. In the six years they've lived here, they've always paid on the first of the month, so let's wait a while to see what happens. Let's not embarrass them."

Pinsk-born Shimon Davis was a carpenter by trade. His wife's relatives had helped them come to Springfield in the early 1900s, and eventually he'd made enough money to be able to purchase the house on Allendale Street. It was a big three-story house with two apartments in the upper stories. The Horowitzes lived on the second floor and Mr. and Mrs. Goldman on the third.

In those days, paying off a mortgage seemed to take forever; the monthly payments went to paying off the interest on the principal without ever chipping away at the actual loan. Sometime in the late 1920s, a law was passed stating that holders of mortgages would have to start paying on the principal in addition to paying the interest. This was very difficult for Papa Davis to do. Times were hard and jobs scarce. As a self-employed carpenter, all his work came through personal recommendations, and he was barely eking out a living. It was only the rent money from his two tenants that enabled him to meet the mortgage payments every month.

One day, Rochele was standing in the kitchen helping her mother clean cherries for the basement barrel of cherry brandy when Mr. and Mrs. Goldman walked in. Their expressions were downcast.

"It's hard for us to have to tell you this," Mr. Goldman began, "but last week I lost my job and I won't be able to pay the rent for this month. I'm afraid we are going to have to move."

Papa Davis did not blink an eye as he said in a voice full of empathy, "Mr. Goldman, it's not the end of the world. If you have your health and a good wife, you have every reason to feel like a wealthy man. You can't move now. Where would you go? Everybody is having a hard time now. Stay here and help me fix the house. We have so many things that need fixing and Fayge just asked me about a new paint job. Your work will be the payment for the rent. In the meantime, you can look for a job. G-d will help and times will get better. You are like family, and family sticks together, so don't move now."

Mr. Goldman looked at his landlord — and friend — in amazement. "But Mr. Davis — you folks are having a hard time yourselves. We can't impose on you."

"Don't feel like that," Rochele heard her father answer. "I meant every word I said."

The Goldmans stayed on in the third-floor apartment for

another year. Mr. Goldman did chores around the house and yard work as well. After that rent-less year, he told Mr. Davis that he just couldn't continue with the arrangement. He and his wife would move to his sister's farm.

Both families shed tears at the emotional farewell, for the bond they had formed was a close one.

The Goldman's apartment was vacant but not for long. So many of Papa Davis's friends were jobless and homeless that the apartment filled up quickly. This often made him the object of criticism, with people saying, "Are you so rich that you can afford to let people stay with you rent-free?"

But he had his answer ready: "How can I have a roof over my head while my people are out in the cold? The *Aibishter* will help."

A year passed. One day when Rochele came home from first grade, she was surprised to see her father at home. He was sitting at the kitchen table with his tea and his sugar cubes. He handed his daughter a sugar cube, kissed her on the forehead, and asked her to please go see if the pussycat had fresh water. As Rochele walked out of the kitchen she heard her father say sadly, "Fayge, I'm going to the bank this afternoon to tell the manager that I don't have the money for both the principal and the mortgage. I don't know what he's going to tell me, so we have to be prepared to sell the house."

As she walked her husband to the front door, his wife told him, "Whatever will be, Shimon, you should know that money or no money, this house is a house of mitzvos. G-d will help us."

Papa walked down the front path very slowly. Just as he was about to turn into the street, the mailman stopped him.

"Mr. Davis, I have a very thick envelope for you." Mr. Davis took it back into the house and put it on the table.

"Fayge, here's the mail."

He turned to leave and was halfway down the path when suddenly his wife cried, "Shimon! Shimon!"

Alarmed, Mr. Davis ran back into the house. There he saw his wife standing in the front hall, and in her hands, the opened envelope — filled with five- and ten-dollar bills.

"Shimon! The Goldmans sent us a whole year's rent money — and they want to know if the apartment is vacant so they can move back!"

Singing all the way and thanking Hashem for the miracle, Papa Davis took the money to the bank to pay the mortgage.

On Wings of Inspiration

People often come up with good ideas but think to themselves, "I could never take on such a big project," or, "It may be a great idea but it would take an organization to put it into practice." Not so Clara Hammer, the chicken lady of Jerusalem. She didn't wait for hesitation and doubt to paralyze her into inaction. She acted immediately. Once her project took off, it received the support of family, friends, and eventually, the international community.

It all started 15 years ago when Mrs. Hammer went to the butcher shop to buy chickens for Shabbos. She walked inside and took her place in line behind a young girl of about 12. The child's long hair was neatly braided, and she wore a blue skirt with a flowered blouse, the usual attire for ultra-Orthodox girls in

Jerusalem. Mrs. Hammer's curiosity was aroused, though, when she saw the butcher hand the girl a large plastic bag filled with nothing but chicken fat and skin. The girl took the bag, said a polite thank-you, and walked out.

After the girl had left the store, Mrs. Hammer asked the butcher, "How many dogs or cats does that family have?"

"No, *Geveret* Hammer," the butcher shook his head slowly, "that family does not have dogs or cats. The father is on dialysis and there are seven children in the family. They owe me 10,000 *lirot* and I just can't give them any more meat on credit. I save this stuff especially for them, to give it to them for free."

Mrs. Hammer was appalled. "You consider yourself a religious man, don't you?"

"I should hope so."

"Well," said Mrs. Hammer emphatically, "you are giving that family poison! You know why you have all this junk left over? Because nobody wants to eat it. I wouldn't even feed it to an animal! So from now on, please, do not give it to that girl and her family. You give them two chickens every week, or one chicken and the equivalent of another chicken — it can be some chopped meat or hot dogs for the children — and put it on my bill."

Word spread to other needy families and before she knew it, Mrs. Hammer was providing Shabbos chickens for four families. As a retired Hebrew teacher living on social security, however, Mrs. Hammer knew she had reached the limit of what she personally could handle. Yet she didn't have the heart to think of families sitting down to an impoverished Shabbos table. Why, Shabbos was supposed to be a day of joy and plenty! How could the children enjoy themselves if there wasn't anything special to eat?

She enlisted the support of her children and grandchildren, and convinced friends and neighbors to contribute, too. Vegetarian families were provided with soy schnitzel and other similar products. "Why should some people be deprived," she said with an understanding chuckle, "just because they don't eat chicken?"

Over the years Mrs. Hammer's project grew, yet it remained a one-woman operation. Last year she personally wrote 847 letters to contributors. She wrote so much that her thumb cartilage began to wear out; now she wears a specially designed pad when she writes to give her thumb muscles a chance to heal. A close friend once said to her, "Clara, don't be ridiculous. Get a computer and then you'll be able to push a button and send everyone the same letter. You have to spare your thumb."

"What you don't understand," Mrs. Hammer told her friend, "is that a Rabbi is not the same as a business executive, and *he's* not the same as a young teenage boy who traveled here for the summer, and *he's* not the same as a girl who just had her bas mitzvah. How can I send everyone the same letter? That's nonsense!"

Here is one letter Mrs. Hammer received from a young girl attending a school in Cleveland:

> Dear Clara Hammer,
> Hi! My name is Aliza Greenberg. I just became bat mitzvah and I want to give charity to an organization but I want to know about it first. Please write back telling me what your organization does and where the money goes. Thank you for your help and cooperation.
> Sincerely,
> Aliza Greenberg

The same day the letter came in the mail, Mrs. Hammer penned her reply:

Dear Aliza Greenberg,

Mazel tov to you on your bat mitzvah! Mazel tov to your parents, who made you a bat mitzvah, and to the Rabbis and the principal whose names appear on your letter. I want to tell you, I am not an organization. I do not have an office. I don't even have a computer. I hand-write each letter, just like I'm writing to you. Last year I wrote 847 letters. I'm sending you a paper that will tell you all about my chicken fund. I go to the post office, I pay for the stamps, I go to the printing shop to print up material, I go to the butcher every week to pay him. Each stamp is two shekels; I pay for them. I buy forty at a time. Two of my great-grandchildren just had their bar mitzvahs. I didn't buy myself a new dress. I wear what I have. I give things up for this *tzedakah* fund because when I sit down Friday night or Shabbos during the day and I eat a piece of chicken or whatever, it tastes doubly good because I know that 314 children from 91 families also have either a piece of chicken or a meatball or sometimes a little hot dog. It means a lot to me to know that other people have what to eat. Of course, I get a lot of help. I couldn't do it on my own. I have between 250 and 300 contributors from the United States, Canada, England, and now also from *Eretz Yisrael*. So any charity you send will go for those purposes.

Give my regards to the principal and to your teachers who teach you about giving *tzedakah*, which is what the Rambam taught us all to do.

Todah rabbah and Shalom from Jerusalem,
Clara Hammer

Handwritten letters are only one aspect of Clara

Hammer's insistence on a personal touch. She has gone far, far beyond the norm to reach out to a contributor and say thank-you. Once, for instance, she received a check in the mail from America without a return address on the envelope, only the contributor's name. What could she do? How could she thank the benefactor? She decided to photocopy the check and enclose it along with a note to the bank it was drawn on, the Bank of America in Los Angeles, explaining the situation to the bank's manager. She wrote that perhaps the person deliberately withheld a return address because he wanted to remain anonymous. If she did not get a reply from the bank, she would assume that to be the case. But if the lack of return address was an oversight, would the manager please be so kind as to notify his client and ask him to contact Clara Hammer.

The manager complied with her request and soon she received a letter from the California gentleman thanking her for taking the trouble to write the bank in order to thank him!

People are so taken by Mrs. Hammer's honesty and sincerity that they are moved to reach out to make contact with her. She never disappoints them, no matter how unexpected their "visit" might be. One night, for instance, while she was in a deep sleep, Mrs. Hammer's phone rang. She woke with a start and looked at her watch. It was 3:30 a.m. Certain the ringing phone was only a wrong number; Clara turned over to go back to sleep. But the ringing persisted. Now worried that it might be an emergency call from her family in America, she picked up the receiver.

A man's voice came over the line saying, "Hello, can I please speak to the chicken lady?"

"Sir," Mrs. Hammer responded without missing a beat, "you are speaking to the chicken lady at 3:30 in the morning!"

"Oh my goodness, I'm so sorry," came the contrite answer. "I'm calling from Oklahoma City and I didn't realize our time zones are different."

With her classic humor Mrs. Hammer quipped back, "So what do you want, a chicken?"

"No," he laughed. "My name is Jimmy and I want to send you money. I saw that article about you on the Internet, but they didn't print your address."

Mrs. Hammer gave him her address and said, "Okay Jim, you can give my phone number to anybody who sends checks. And don't worry, they can wake me up anytime of the night." Jim from Oklahoma City sent a check and an apology. He also promised that part of his paycheck would always go to Mrs. Hammer's Chicken Fund in Jerusalem.

"I don't need any thanks," Mrs. Hammer declares emphatically. "I love Hashem with all my heart and all my soul and I try to do this work with *emunah* and with love. With everything I witnessed in my childhood in Europe, and all the miracles Hashem did for me, I must in some small way say thank-you."

Now in her 90s, Mrs. Hammer is and always has been a woman of conviction and action. She never was one to wait for people to ask for help before pitching in wholeheartedly. And you can be sure it doesn't stop with chickens. Countless *brisos* made, clothing and furniture for the needy collected, nursery-school toys provided, Shabbos candles donated — all this and more awaited her as she stood on line that landmark day in the butcher shop. How different the lives of so many people — her own included — would have been had Mrs. Clara Hammer not donated that first chicken.

Read more about Mrs. Hammer below.

Poor Shula

The greatness of a person is best revealed by his everyday behavior, by his seemingly small acts of kindness, by his willingness to rise to the occasion. Once again, Clara Hammer, unpretentious as ever, shows us how a caring heart and a willingness to give can be put into action without any fanfare.

One day during the Yom Kippur War, Clara Hammer was sitting on a bench enjoying the fresh air when she overheard a conversation taking place between two women she didn't know. They were commiserating over their neighbor's situation.

"Poor Shula. She just came home from the hospital with triplets and she has two other little children. Her husband was called up to the army, and her mother, who planned on coming to help, just came down with pneumonia and is in the hospital. I just don't know how Shula's going to manage."

Mrs. Hammer was up in a flash, "Excuse me, I could not help but overhear your conversation. Where does this Shula live?"

The women looked at her questioningly. Who was she and why had she been listening to their conversation?

Undaunted, Clara persisted, "Well, I would be glad to help her. Where does she live?"

Why not? they thought. "Right around the corner, number 47."

"Thank you. What is her last name?"

"Berger."

Clara picked up her knitting bag and went right over. A knock at the door brought a very tired-looking young woman to the door. A quick glance took in the two toddlers clinging to the mother's skirt. In the background a chorus of newborn cries could be heard.

"Mazel tov, Shula!" said Mrs. Hammer with genuine joy. Shula remained standing in the doorway, looking puzzled and wondering where the kind stranger who stood on her doorstep had come from.

"My name is Clara Hammer," said Mrs. Hammer as if in answer to the unspoken questions. "I live a few blocks away and I can come any time you need help with the children."

Shula stood there speechless. It seemed too good to be true. Overcome, she managed to get out one word. "Really?"

Clara's reply came without any hesitation. "That's right."

What Shula needed the most help with was feeding the babies. She could only feed two at a time, and of course that was exactly when her toddlers decided they needed an extra dollop of mommy's attention. She gave Mrs. Hammer a schedule of the triplets' feeding times, and from that moment on, every day at meal time "Savta Clara" was there.

When the war was over and Shula's husband returned from the front, the grateful couple presented Mrs. Hammer with a beautiful *siddur*. Over the years the two families kept in touch, so it was with a deep sense of closeness that Clara participated in a triply happy bar-mitzvah celebration.

As Mrs. Hammer so matter-of-factly puts it, "Some people listen and say, 'Oh, poor Shula.' What do you mean 'poor Shula'?! At that time, I didn't yet have my great-grandchildren. I was willing and able, so why shouldn't I help someone instead of just sitting on a bench?"

Just think: If the other two women had gotten off the bench instead of talking about "poor Shula," each one of the triplets would have had someone to hold him.

A Pact Between Sisters

Mrs. Leila David had to help out with the household finances. She did not have any choice but to work to contribute to the expense. Luckily she loved her job as a receptionist for a mid-sized Manhattan firm. She also loved being with her children, and so she gave them extra special attention when she came home. How she would have loved to stay home and raise her family, but it just wasn't possible. Now, though, she was faced with a crisis: the loss of their beloved "Nana." Her dependable housekeeper, so much a part of the family for all these years, was moving to Florida. Without a replacement, Leila was sure she would lose her job immediately.

Leila walked over to her sister's apartment on Manhattan's Upper West Side, her heart heavy and her mind spinning. Should she let herself be fired from her job, and stay at home? But they needed the extra income! Yet Nana was leaving. Nana was like a grandmother to the children. Why, she had been with them for over seven years! Who could ever replace her? Nana's husband's asthma had taken a turn for the worse, and that's why she had given such sudden notice about the move to Florida. With winter quickly approaching, they were making arrangements to leave as soon as possible.

As she knocked on her sister's door, Leila just couldn't contain herself any longer and as soon as Miriam opened the door, Leila burst into tears.

"What's the matter? Is everything all right? Why are you crying?"

"Oh, Miriam — Nana is leaving us. She's moving to Florida because of Joe's asthma."

"My goodness, that's nothing to get so worked up over. You made me nervous. Don't worry, you'll find another maid."

"She's not just a maid, she's a Nana. Nobody can ever replace her!"

Miriam sat Leila down with a cup of hot tea and cake, trying to get her to relax.

"You see," Leila explained to her sister, "I have no leeway. I used up all my vacation time and sick leave after Yaakov's birth. He's only two months old now. I could take an unpaid leave of absence, but my boss told me that if I do, there's no guarantee that my position will stay open. You know how much I need my job. How I wish I could be like you, staying at home, cooking and baking and cleaning and playing with the children. Your house is always sparkling, and the children are always so happy."

"Leila, I have an idea," said Miriam with mounting excitement. "Maybe it will sound a bit strange, but we might be able to work out the details. You're right, I can stay at home and you have to work. You need someone to take care of your kids and I can always use the extra income — so why not let them come to me! I can't clean your house — you'll have to hire someone else to do that. But my twins and Moshe will be very happy to have their cousins to play with every day."

"Miriam, that's a great idea. But do you really think it will work?"

"Why not? At the very least we could try it for a few months and then decide. In the meantime, it will take the pressure off you."

The sisters put their plan into action. It worked so well that Miriam raised her nieces and nephews along with her own six children. Both now grandmothers, the two sisters often reminisce about how their children shared everything, right down to measles and chickenpox. Leila advanced in her firm to the position of managing director. As for the cousins, although they've branched out all over the world, they are all still unusually close. You might say, they're just like brothers and sisters.

❧ Heaven-sent Chavrusah

Mrs. Nechama Klein was always the mainstay of the family, ever since she was a little girl. Her mother had given her that responsibility before she passed away. "Nechama'le," she had said, "after I die, you have to take care of everyone and keep the family together." Nechama was faithful to her mother's wish, even after she was married and had a family of her own. It was in her home that the Chanukah parties and Pesach Seders for the extended family, numbering over 50 people, took place. Despite having to nurse her husband through a 16-year-long battle with a cancer diagnosed when he was only 35, and even though they couldn't afford it, Nechama kept everyone together. At the bar-mitzvah celebration for one of her grandsons, Mrs. Klein, now well into her 70s, spoke into the video.

"I am a very wealthy woman. I have fifteen grandsons who are Torah Jews. These are my diamonds and these are my pearls."

Shortly thereafter, she was taken ill with a crippling disease. Her children were suddenly faced with a fateful decision: Should they or shouldn't they follow her doctor's advice to try an experimental medication not yet approved by the FDA? What follows is the story of how they received Divine guidance to help them make their decision.

After extensive testing, the doctors found the source of Mrs. Klein's symptoms: a brain tumor that had apparently been growing for quite a few years. Her children were faced with the unknown, and finding it hard to deal with. The medical experts told them point blank, "If you do nothing, her time is limited, maybe two or three months at the most. If we operate and try to take out as much as we can, she may live a little longer, and her time will be quality time."

The family was distraught. They asked Torah authorities, and were told that they had to try the operation, because it did offer a possibility of prolonging her life.

Mrs. Klein underwent the operation, and it was partially successful. The surgeons weren't able to remove all of the growth, though. At that point, the family was informed that they had to make a decision about the course of treatment. "Regular chemotherapy drugs have been on the market for over 20 years," the neurosurgeon told them, "and their success rate with brain tumors is not as good as we would like, especially with the elderly. But there is a new drug, and we would like to give it a try with your mother. It is a new development, so only about 100 patients have tried it, but so far, the results have been encouraging. Given the statistics for regular chemotherapy," he concluded, "I'd say we have nothing to lose."

Her children didn't know what to do. Both prospects looked bleak.

The day after the family was presented with this decision, David, Nechama's third son, went to *kollel* as usual. His *chavrusah* could not help but notice the depressed and distraught mood of his usually cheerful friend and asked him if there was any way he could be of help. David told him about the decision facing the family. He explained briefly that they were being asked to choose a course of treatment after their mother's brain surgery, and that they were debating whether to stick to traditional chemotherapy or to follow her doctor's suggestion to try a new experimental drug.

"Before I even present the case to a Rav," said David wearily, "I'll need to get more information."

"I have an idea," said his *chavrusah*. "My brother-in-law is in family medicine in Chicago. He used to be an oncologist, but a few years ago he switched his specialty. Why don't you call him, tell him who you are, say that we're close friends and that I gave you his number. Maybe he can give you some good advice."

David called Chicago, and told his *chavrusah*'s brother-in-law the story. The reply he got was one he could never have imagined.

"Although I am not a religious man," began Dr. Goldman, "right now I have goosebumps all over."

"What are you talking about?" asked David.

"Nothing ever happens purely by chance. But here you are calling me from New York, out of the blue, to tell me about your mother and an experimental drug and my hair is standing on end."

David was just as confused as ever. "I still don't understand," he said.

"I was the one who did the research on that drug in New York!" the Chicago physician practically screamed into the phone. "I was the one, along with a co-worker, who discovered it three years ago. Don't use it — it doesn't work."

"Then why," asked David, "is the doctor pressing us to use this drug?"

"Listen," came the answer, this time in a more subdued tone. "he may pin hopes on it as a last resort. I can't let you use my name, so don't tell anyone you got this information from me, but I am telling you loud and clear, don't use that drug. It doesn't work."

David was overwhelmed. He had been feeling too depressed to go to *kollel*. Now he felt that he had been rewarded for pushing himself to go.

The night before the surgery, David and his two sisters had sat outside the hospital room discussing what to do about their mother's care during her recovery period. They were all in full agreement. Upon entering their mother's room David took his mother's hand. The two sisters held each others' hands as well. David spoke softly, his voice catching. "Mama," he said, "we are making you a promise. No matter what, we will never leave you alone."

For the next three years, one of her children always remained at her bedside, day and night.

"How Do You Stay So Thin?"

When Mrs. Green is not managing the family-owned dry-cleaning enterprise, she can be found organizing fund-raising drives for needy brides in her midwestern community. During her childhood and much of her early adult life, Mrs. Green suffered from family and social pressure to lose weight. Now the mother of five grown children who are a credit to their family and the community, she balks at the amount of time and energy she once spent trying to change her physical appearance. "Acceptance is the secret to happiness," she confided in me as we walked home from a lecture one evening, and she told me this story.

Several years ago, Pessie Green bumped into a former classmate, Reeva, in a department store downtown. They hadn't seen each other in quite a while. Their conversation was casual at first, but eventually they started catching up on more significant events. Reeva had always been tall and thin, while Pessie had always been the size she is now, short and round. And Reeva, now the mother of five, the oldest of whom is 14, has stayed the same size she was when they knew each other at the age of 18.

Pessie was surprised and sorry to hear Reeva say that the past year had been a very difficult one for her family. She would never have guessed from looking at her that she is practically house-bound, caring for both her husband *and* her elderly father. It seems that her husband was diagnosed with a rare form of Parkinson's and, as if that wasn't enough, at the same time, her father, who's in his 80s, fell and broke his hip. To add to the burden, her oldest daughter, who is usually a very big help, recently broke her right arm.

As they stood there between the suits and the new arrivals, Pessie couldn't get over how good Reeva looked despite her added responsibilities and suffering. And Reeva didn't have even a trace of bitterness in her voice as she spoke.

"You know, Pessie," she said, "I'm not telling you this so that you'll feel sorry for me. These are the circumstances of my life right now and I'm sharing them with you. But there is one thing that absolutely irks me no end." She paused and hesitated as if trying to decide whether or not to say what was really in her heart. "I know that in our childhood we used to talk a lot about weight and things like that."

"That's for sure," Pessie affirmed. "I was always jealous of your metabolism. You could eat anything and it never showed, while all I had to do was *look* at a piece of cake and I would gain weight!"

"Well, Pessie," said Reeva, her eyes filling with tears, "I want you to know that I just get so angry when people ask me how I stay so thin. Look — I *have* to be strong. I'm taking care of people in my family who are basically invalids.

I have to push wheelchairs and lift them. It's a full-time job, nursing my father and husband. I don't have any bitterness in my heart, honestly. But even in our world, where we know what real values are, this emphasis on the shape of a person's body has really gotten out of hand. This is the body that Hashem gave me. Can we know why? Maybe one of the reasons I'm so tall and strong is so that I can take care of a husband with Parkinson's disease.

"People don't know how to separate the essential from the superficial until circumstances free them to look at life from a fresh perspective. Sure, I appreciate having been born with this body shape. But who's dictating these rules? Where does the Torah talk about being tall and thin? I guess everyone likes to hear that they look good and I know I'm no exception, but really, Pessie, we have to *daven* to be healthy and strong, outside and inside."

As Pessie Green drove home from the department store she couldn't get over her friend's strength of character. Reeva did not have one trace of anger in her heart about her circumstances. What angered her was the illusion of American culture of which even religious women are victims. Reeva's beauty is a true beauty, she thought. Would I be able to bear her life circumstances with the same grace? she wondered. As she thought of people and resources she could contact to help Reeva, Pessie felt very uplifted by their conversation. She might spend hours each week listening to inspirational tapes while she folded laundry, but this one department-store conversation touched a very deep place in her heart.

Kindness / 195

❦ *We Were the Poor Relatives*

Rebbetzin Sheindel Weinbach's description of her childhood years in America of the 40s and 50s is an oral history of her mother's sacrifice for her husband's learning and her children's education. As we watch the portrait develop before our eyes, we can gain a fresh perspective on things we today assume to be the norm. Who knows to what extent the quiet hidden determination of people like the Rebbetzin's mother influenced the direction of Jewish observance in America? Her actions, and those of women like her, formed the infrastructure of our thriving mitzvah-observant community today.

Sheindel Weinbach, nee Sylvie Lamm, was in an orphanage until the end of the war, when she was sent to live with her grandparents in America. "When my grandfather passed away," she now remembers, "it was a toss-up where I should go. But my aunt and uncle, Mr. and Mrs. Lamm, took me in. The fact that they were even in America was a miracle. The truth is, they are very much my mother and father because they raised me." Here, in her own words, she describes her home:

"My aunt, Mrs. Lamm, sat behind her sewing machine at least 18 hours a day. That's how she made a living because while my uncle was in the diamond business, he is best remembered sitting with a pile of *sefarim* in the dining room. Sixty years ago in America this was a very unusual place to be.

"My aunt was born in a small town in Germany to hardworking, yet poor, parents. They, like many of their contemporaries, felt that you could be a full participant in secular culture and still be a loyal Jew. There was no concept of dedicating one's life to Torah and there was certainly no such thing as a *kollel* in their community.

"As a child, she felt the sting of poverty. She braved the fierce German winters with a hat that was too small and often wore no scarf. The *goyishe* children used to chase her and her friends, throwing snowballs that landed on the exposed skin between their hats and jacket collars.

"There wasn't any Bais Yaakov education for the girls. All their values and strength of character came from the home.

"My father met my mother (actually my uncle met my aunt) while he was still in yeshivah. He was born into a very wealthy Belgian family and was expected to go into the family diamond business. Instead of going to college, though, he weathered the disapproval of his entire family and went to yeshivah in Frankfurt. My mother, who was working as a governess then, really liked the idea of somebody who had this spiritual side, who saw beyond society and cultures and norms.

"Right after they married, the war broke out. They had very difficult years running from one place to another. Finally they fled from France to Cuba. On the boat over there, under the worst circumstances, my mother took care of other people. She went from one person to the next, making sure they had food. If someone was sick, she stayed up to take care of them. She had this knack for tuning in to people. Even if she disagreed with them, they knew she would understand. Later on, when she was a seamstress, people would bring her work just to hear her practical advice or to have a sympathetic listening ear. I never knew whom I would find in our tiny house when I came home from school.

"My grandparents had made it to America first, while my mother and father had waited in Cuba a long time because of the quota restrictions. When they were finally able to come, they took a tiny apartment near the rest of the family. My father's older brother lived with his wife and two children in a spacious apartment in the same building. He was very successful in business and they were well-off, while my parents had a studio apartment, with just a kitchen and a living room, where they slept.

"When the question came up of what to do with me, the orphan, it was they who automatically took me in. For them it wasn't even a question. I slept in the kitchen for two or three years. But all along I said *baruch Hashem* it turned out like this. My cousins in the building, who were so well-off, were sent to public school, while my aunt and uncle, who really did not have the money, made sure that I got a proper Jewish day-school education, right along with their own children. They worked very hard, and begged the administration for reduced tuition. All these sacrifices were made in a very beautiful spirit, even though it made them the target of family ridicule. They sent us to a Jewish day school, and every summer, we went to Camp Bais Yaakov. Our high-school years were spent at Bais Yaakov High School.

"Once when we went downstairs to visit our cousins, their parents said to my mother, 'Our children know *berachos*, they can *daven*, they go to Hebrew school in the afternoon — what more do we need? They are only girls.'

"We had two elderly great-aunts, my grandmother's sisters, who were from the old school of high society in Belgium. They were at odds with us all the time but my mother taught us to show them respect. We would visit them once a week, and sit in the parlor drinking the coke they knew my mother allowed.

"When the question of higher education came up, the arguments were horrible. 'You're ruining these girls,' they would tell my mother. 'You're turning them into recluses! Why do you want to go and waste money you don't even have on a religious education?'

"No one can imagine the social pressure there was because we were the 'poor relatives.' We wore hand-me-down clothing given by the very same relatives who criticized us.

"But my mother was very strong. How many women in our neighborhood at that time, even very *frum* women, covered their hair? Only a handful — and my mother was one of them. It wasn't that she didn't care what other people thought. She cared deeply. But she overcame her feelings in favor of doing the right thing.

"Even when we came home from high school with religious ideas she had never heard of, she listened with an open mind and was willing to change. For example, 40 years ago in America the idea of *kollel* was completely foreign. Likewise, the idea of a simple lifestyle. We would tell her about our teacher who used to say, 'Why do we need fancy flowers at a wedding? Put a note on the table saying the money was donated to charity.' My mother thought these things over carefully.

"In America, even in the early days, she belonged to the *chevrah kaddisha*. And remember, this was a person who needed every penny. But when the burial society called, she dropped everything to go. When she returned home, she would sit and cry. Especially if it had been a young woman who had passed away.

"Watching her over the years, we definitely learned that life was much more than sitting behind a sewing machine."

Partners in Life

Let's Build a Family

In these times when the family unit is beset by so many internal and external stresses, it is extremely heartening to read about how Omi (that's German for grandmother), who lost her daughter, and Lena, who lost her husband, rebuilt their lives together through Lena's marriage to Omi's son-in-law, Michael. As Lena tells it, "It wasn't just a marriage of two; we were bringing together 11 people. And Omi had been taking care of her son-in-law and grandchildren for a few years. It was a situation fraught with pitfalls right from the start. But, baruch Hashem, we found favor in each other's eyes."

Let us learn from this extraordinary family how to see the good in others and cultivate positive relationships through giving of ourselves.

Lena had just arrived in Belgium. She walked up the steps to the big brick house with excitement and trepidation. She was just about to meet her future mother-in-law. Actually, she was inheriting a mother-in-law. Who'd ever heard of such a strange thing? But such is life. Her husband-to-be, a widower, was still very close to his departed wife's mother, the grandmother of his five small children.

Lena paused before knocking on the imposing door. Her own four children stood alongside her. As she lifted the shiny brass knocker, she couldn't tell which was colder, her fingers or the brass.

It had been a difficult and lonely three years. Lena had been a happily married mother of four children. She had been working as an architect for a kitchen design firm. She was very grateful that after the initial consultation with the client, most of her work could be done at home. And then, in her early 30s, her world was shattered. Her husband was killed in a sudden tragic accident.

Being a person of strong faith, Lena was determined to carry on and raise her children with as much love and devotion as possible. For the first two years, she was certain she would never marry again. Then Divine providence brought her distant cousins from Belgium for a visit and they told her about Michael.

He had lost his wife three years earlier, right around the time her husband was killed. His mother-in-law had moved in during the period of her daughter's illness to take care of her and the five children. Now, she was still living with them and running the household.

"It sounds so complicated," Lena said. "It is a situation that is fraught with difficulty right from the start."

But her cousins were persistent, and six months later she found herself in the midst of an international *shidduch*. When Lena became engaged and decided to uproot her family to move to Belgium, she knew that it was not a joining of just two people — it was a marriage of 11!

On the flight from Chicago to Antwerp she had tried to explain the circumstances in greater detail to her children.

"Omi is their Granny," Lena had explained to her children, as the plane glided along the mid-afternoon sunlit sky. "In fact, that's what Omi means in German: grandmother. Their mother died right around the same time that Daddy was killed in the accident."

Now she stood with her hand on the knocker. Michael was coming in a few hours for their very first "family dinner." Lena took a deep breath and knocked on the door.

It was answered by an elegant, impeccably dressed woman in her mid-60s. After a warm handshake, Omi immediately gave the children some candy and introduced them to the rest of their soon-to-be new siblings.

"Come, dear," said Omi to Lena. "Let's let them play in the other room while we get acquainted. Would you like a cup of tea?"

For the next three hours, Omi and Lena sat and talked. They forged an instant bond.

Omi had grown up in Germany, near the Dutch border, where she married at the age of 29. Her three children were born during World War II, while the family was in hiding in France. After the war, they traveled to the Jewish community in Lyons, which had been totally devastated. Young as she was then, Omi was hired to care for the *mikveh* and joined the *chevrah kaddisha* (burial society). She was the sort of person who — when something needed to be done, and no one else was forthcoming — jumped right in.

When Omi was widowed at the age of 49, she decided not to remarry until her children were grown up and settled in their own homes. Before this took place, her daughter, Helen, became ill, and Omi moved in to care for her and the family.

Omi was a fantastic cook and an excellent homemaker. By nature and training she was a calm relaxed person who never became flustered or lost her temper. So, although the children had to cope with the terrible suffering of their mother's illness and her subsequent death, Omi was always there with her delicious food, her soothing influence and her comforting words.

After they had exchanged stories, there was a lull in the conversation. In the midst of the silence, Omi put her hand on Lena's arm and said, "This is not going to be easy for either one of us, dear, but let's work together and build a family."

And that is what they did. After the wedding, Omi and Lena sat down together to discuss logistics.

"Omi," Lena began, "I don't want our children to forget that they had another mother and another father. How about if Michael and I are called *"Abba"* and *"Ima,"* while the parents who are no longer alive remain Mommy and Daddy. This way the children will be free to talk about them. We will keep their pictures out, too."

Omi was in complete agreement. "Yes," she sighed, "that would be best for the children."

Lena wasn't sure how her next point would be received, but she knew she had to voice her concerns right from the start.

"Omi," she continued, "there's one thing that I'm very concerned about. In Chicago, I was a working mother. Cooking was never number one on my agenda; spending time with my children took priority. We were very happy with cheese sandwiches and fresh salad. But here, in your household, everything is very formal. The food is always perfectly prepared and very beautifully served. The children have been spoiled with such good food and I won't be able to live up to those standards"

Omi gave Lena a look of compassion.

"Don't worry, Lena," she said reassuringly, "I'll teach you and I'll help you."

True to her word, for the next 18 years Omi came over almost every day to help her son-in-law's new wife manage the household of 11. She and Lena worked in the kitchen as a team, sharing recipes and techniques, doing all the cooking and baking together.

Everyone who knew them marveled at their relationship.

"You can well imagine," Lena recalls, "how I felt. Omi was a constant reminder of my husband's first wife. In the beginning, this was very difficult for me. I felt my capabilities as a housewife and mother were constantly being judged. But Omi wasn't the sort to make you feel inadequate. That was what was so special about her.

"Michael wasn't even her own son, and my children were total strangers. But we all realized that it was to our mutual benefit that Omi remain close to the family. She was just so good to have around. And then Ilana was born and she and Omi got along fabulously. It all took time, but it was a genuine bonding. Omi became a real grandmother to my natural children, right down to never forgetting their birthdays.

"Omi always came with us on vacations. My natural children considered her their grandmother and she always came to their *simchahs*. They treat her other children as aunts and uncles. My 'super-natural' children — as I like to call the children that came with the marriage — treat my late husband's family as their family. We all became very, very close.

"Early in our marriage, my husband and I went to Switzerland for a vacation. He wanted to buy me a very expensive gold necklace but I felt uncomfortable about it. It wasn't that we couldn't afford it. *Baruch Hashem,* we can afford many things that I just don't buy because that is not my style. But my husband insisted.

"When we arrived home, I kept wondering what Omi would say. I didn't know if Michael had ever bought his first wife such a beautiful necklace.

"I walked in and, after saying hello, Omi noticed the necklace and said, 'Lena, it's about time you had a decent piece of jewelry. Wear it in good health!'

"That was Omi — she had no pettiness in her, just goodness and a generosity of spirit."

Outside of caring for the family, Omi led quite an active life. She had many friends, and even in her early 80s she would go to the nursing home to visit "the old people" — some of whom were younger than she was!

It wasn't always smooth sailing for either Lena or Omi. In the beginning especially, Lena bent over backwards to bond with her "super-natural" children. One night, one of her own daughters came to her and said, "Ima, I know you have to be fair, but do you have to be *so* fair?"

One of the younger boys was extremely hyperactive and had multiple learning problems. As a result, he appeared to Lena to be very spoiled and she felt he needed discipline. There were times — such as when she would not let him have supper until he put his toys away — that she knew she seemed too strict with him. She never quite knew whether Omi approved or disapproved of her handling of him. Only years later, on the day of that child's wedding, Omi said to her as they drove to the reception, "Lena, you worked wonders with that boy. He was such a high-spirited child, I never knew how he was going to turn out!"

Omi's health began to fail when she reached her mid-80s. Lena and Michael wouldn't hear of putting her into a nursing home and they insisted she come to live with them. The families pooled their resources and made a plan for round-the-clock care. During her final days, Omi lost consciousness, yet somehow remained acutely aware of who was caring for her. She loved Ilana and she would accept a drink of water only from her.

The night before she died, Ilana was with her. Ilana opened the *siddur* and noticed that the page she opened to was the *Shema* that one says before death. She decided to say it softly. That next day, Tuesday, Lena was with Omi in the afternoon when she died quietly, holding Lena's hand. The one who had given so much of herself during her lifetime had been enveloped in a cocoon of love and kindness right to her very last breath.

This wasn't a fantasy family — this was a family of real people, with all the struggles that real people go through. Perhaps more than anything the following incident sums up their approach:

When Ilana, who was everybody's natural sister, was about three or four years old, she began to realize that they were two families. Not that Lena or Michael had ever hidden anything; it was just that she became aware that there had been another Mommy and another Daddy before her Abba and Ima.

Ilana began to ask questions. "Is she yours or Abba's?" she would ask her mother intently about one of her sisters, trying to put all the pieces into place, slowly beginning to understand the concept of certain siblings being related to each other by marriage.

Then one day she asked about Omi. "Omi," answered her mother truthfully, "is not your real grandmother."

Ilana was devastated. She ran upstairs to the room she shared with her sisters.

Because she adored Omi, the little girl was determined to understand how the older woman fit into her life. After thinking it over up in her room, she came back downstairs to her mother and said, "You know what, Ima? Omi is my grandmother by love!"

What made their relationship so successful? "We accepted

each other," says Lena. "We didn't run away from the pain of the past. That it was hard was a given. But right from the start we made a decision: With G–d's help, we will make this work — no matter what."

✍ Loyalty and Devotion: A Gulf War Shabbos

Well-known and beloved, Rabbi and Rebbetzin Schwartz have been serving Klal Yisrael together for many years. Their home is a place where the doorbell and telephone hardly ever stop ringing. The Rav sits surrounded by his sefarim, immersed in learning, with a white cordless telephone a few inches away from his right hand.

The real test of a shepherd comes when his flock is in danger. In this story, the Rav and the Rebbetzin demonstrate their loyalty and devotion to Torah, to each other, and to helping Klal Yisrael at a time when, quite literally, nobody knew what was flying.

Despite the threat and fear of war, *Rosh Chodesh* Shevat began with *simchahs* for the Rav and the Rebbetzin. That night they went to *sheva berachos* for the children of good friends. Upon arriving home they received the good news that a *shidduch* they had arranged, had been finalized. The Rav and Rebbetzin bid each other good night with tremendous happiness. Even the ominous clouds of war hanging over their heads could not diminish their joy over the wonderful news.

Yet sleep did not come easily for the Rebbetzin. Between the excitement of the *simchahs* and her fearful anticipation of war, she no sooner closed her eyes than the terrifying image of a gas mask loomed menacingly. She envisioned her precious grandchildren wrapped up in those protective coats the adults had been instructed to put on them, confined to those hideous plastic cribs.

A few weeks earlier the Rebbetzin had gone with her married daughter to the local school to receive instructions from the soldiers and to watch an hour-long video on the subject of protective measures in the event of an enemy gas attack. She had learned how to put on a black rubber gas mask, how to inject herself with an antidote for gas poisoning, and how to dust special powder on chemical burns. As for the book on chemical warfare, she had brought that home for the Rav to read, because she knew that although he had gone down to pick up the mask, he hadn't watched any of the demonstrations.

"Faygie," he said when he noticed the book in the house, "why did you buy this? We went together to learn about those things."

"Now look, Hershel, you know as well as I do that you weren't paying any attention to those instructions. G–d forbid we should have to make use of it, but I thought we'd better have the book just in case." She looked at her husband and saw that he had a big smile on his face and a twinkle in his eyes.

"You were supposed to be watching that video, not me!" he said in mock accusation.

"Somebody had to keep an eye on you."

"Oh, so now I have my own private eye!"

That had been hours ago, and now as she fought wakefulness, the Rebbetzin knew she had to get some sleep.

Otherwise, she would be unable to function the next morning. She remembered that as a child, whenever she had been very afraid at night, her father would tell her the story about how he was miraculously saved from the Germans.

Her father had been captured by the Germans in World War I. He had been a Polish citizen but they had arrested him anyway and put him in a work camp where he was ordered to paint a bridge. He knew that if he went up on that bridge he would surely fall to his death. He didn't favor dying that way, but he couldn't see any way out. He couldn't climb up on the bridge, but he also couldn't refuse to do the work. He decided instead to try to escape — and he did.

He made it to the forest.

Suddenly a German officer appeared and demanded his papers. He didn't have papers. That meant he was either a spy, or an escaped prisoner. Either way, the German was going to kill him, so he asked if he could just say his prayers before he died. And he was granted this privilege.

He let out a scream at the top of his lungs: "*Shema Yisrael, Hashem Elokeinu, Hashem Echad!*" He started to cry and say *Vidui*. Suddenly, the sound of horses reached their ears. In a flash, German officers galloped into the clearing. They asked the soldier what he was doing with the man. The soldier said he had caught a spy and was going to kill him.

"How do you know he's a spy?" the officers asked. "Let him go — anybody who prays like that can't be a spy!"

The Rebbetzin remembered how her father always ended this story by saying, "You see, Faygele, we always have to do what is right in the eyes of Hashem. Of course we feel afraid sometimes, but *Got vet helfen* (G–d will help)."

The reassuring memory of this story helped the

Rebbetzin put things in perspective. "Faygie," she said to herself, "you are in your own home in your own comfortable bed. The chances of anything actually happening, G–d forbid, are minimal, so now you must go to sleep." Resolved to keep calm, she fell into a deep restful sleep.

At three o'clock in the morning, the ringing of the phone startled her from sleep. It was her daughter. "Hello, Ma, the war's started. Wake up Daddy and turn on the radio. I gotta go before the kids get into the chemicals! I'll talk to you in the morning."

With pounding heart and ice-cold, trembling hands, the Rebbetzin jumped out of bed — and promptly stepped right into her *negel vasser* bowl. After mopping up the water, she switched on the light, turned on the radio, and woke up the Rav, who spent 20 minutes concentrating on the book of chemical warfare and getting his gas mask to fit perfectly — despite the fact that army instructions called for removal of the beard first.

"Cut my beard for a gas mask?" he retorted. "I won't do that."

That night there was no attack, but the atmosphere was very tense. The next night, the siren signaling an attack pierced the night air with a loud, eerie wail. The Rav and the Rebbetzin rushed into their sealed room. The Rav donned his gas mask like a pro, making sure he could breathe and hear the radio. He saw his wife fumbling with the straps, the mask still on her lap.

"Let me show you how to use this thing," he offered. But when she finally got the mask on her face, the Rebbetzin panicked and couldn't breathe. She started screaming, "Help! Get me out of here, I can't breathe," and tore the thing from her face.

"Faygie, what are you doing?"

"I can't breathe in there. If I keep that thing on my face I'll be dead for sure. I'll be the first to go! In the video they said you could use a baking-soda-and-water solution on a towel." The Rebbetzin ran out of the sealed room to the kitchen and quickly prepared a pail with baking soda and water. She ran back into the sealed room and there they sat, the Rav in his mask, with a *sefer* in his hand, the Rebbetzin scared stiff with a wet towel over her face, trying to breathe through a rag. The army radio station played music to calm its listeners. Finally the announcer, his voice that of a master hypnotist, gave the all-clear signal. Thank G-d, no gas, no chemicals, and no loss of life.

At five o'clock in the morning, there was another siren. This time one of the Rav's students called and described what he had seen on the news. The Rebbetzin was terrified. She was wondering how she would maintain her composure when the Friday telephone *shaylahs* began. Friday morning, after very little sleep, she forced herself out of bed.

Over a morning cup of coffee, her husband filled her in on the latest news. "Thank G-d, Faygie, nobody was badly hurt. There was property damage but no major injuries to people, that's the main thing."

"The main thing now is," the Rebbetzin mused to herself, "what am I going to do about *challahs* for Shabbos?" There were no *challahs* in the store, so she would have to bake them herself. But how was she going to bake *challah* with trembling fingers? And what if an air-raid siren went off in the middle of baking? But Shabbos was coming, no two ways about it. She took out the flour, yeast, and all the other ingredients she needed and by nine o'clock in the morning, the *challah* was rising. As soon as she had washed the last bit of dough from her hands, the phone rang. She answered and heard the voice of a person who sounded almost near death.

"Rebbetzin?"

"Is that you, Mrs. Levine? I barely recognized your voice! What's the matter?"

"Rebbetzin, my husband told me that any time from now on there could be another attack because it only takes them seven hours to refuel."

The Rebbetzin felt a wave of utter panic at the thought of that grim possibility, but she answered as calmly as she could, "Mrs. Levine, *Got vet helfen*. G-d is going to help us. He brought us this far and He's not going to abandon us now. The main thing is that we must get ready for Shabbos. If there's an attack, G-d forbid, you'll go straight into your sealed room and everything will be okay."

No sooner had the Rebbetzin put down the phone, when it rang again. "I'm sorry to disturb you, Rebbetzin, but what does the Rav say we should do about the radio on Shabbos?" The Rebbetzin took down the family's name and number, said she would call them back with the Rav's answer, and ran back to her pots. She rushed through her cooking and preparations as fast as possible, for she could tell by the way the morning was shaping up that her main task that *erev Shabbos* would be to man the phones.

The phone rang again. It was Mrs. Moskowitz. "Rebbetzin, I'm not going to make it through another attack. It's too much on my heart." The caller had been on one of the first boats that left America for Israel following World War II. She was in her late 80s and in her third marriage.

"Oh, Mrs. Moskowitz, you've lived through much worse than this. Don't you worry. Just put those nitroglycerin pills right near your gas mask and the *Aibishter vet helfen*."

Just as she hung up, the phone rang again. This time, it

was a new mother. "Rebbetzin, my nerves can't take it. Every time the house creaks, I jump. My baby cried this morning and I thought it was another siren. Rebbetzin, I think I'm cracking up. Do you know the name of a good travel agent? I think I have to get out of here."

"Now, look, Sara'le, go and get some schnapps and put a little in hot water and drink it. It will calm you down. We cannot allow ourselves to be hysterical," she said, remembering how she herself had screamed from behind the gas mask. "*Got vet helfen.*"

By Friday afternoon, it became public knowledge that it was permissible to turn the radio on before Shabbos and leave it on throughout the whole day. To each caller, she repeated the Rav's message to leave the lights on continuously, instead of having the Shabbos clock turn them off. This way, if there was an attack, no one would be caught in a dark apartment, searching for the gas masks.

Thank G-d, the day passed without sirens — and the *challah* looked beautiful. Although the Rav instructed all callers to leave their radios on a low volume, he decided that in his home they would not leave the radio on. *Shabbos kodesh* was *Shabbos kodesh*.

Candlelighting was at 4:30 that day. At 4:15, just as the Rav was about to step out the door to go to *shul*, the phone rang again. It was a close friend from the *shul*. The Rebbetzin watched as her husband's expression grew tense and concerned. "Hershel," she said with nervous excitement, "please tell me, what is it?"

The Rav covered the mouthpiece of the phone and said, "Wolfson's son is in the army and he heard from top-secret sources that this Shabbos, G-d forbid, there will be a terrible attack, something like we have never seen before."

The Rav uncovered the mouthpiece and said, "Okay, Mr.

Wolfson, I'll leave my radio on low, but I must leave for *shul* now. People are expecting me. *Got vet helfen*, it will be all right."

The Rebbetzin could barely stand from fright as she *davened* what she thought might be her last *Minchah*. But as she emerged from the world of prayer, she suddenly felt comforted by the thought of the approaching Shabbos. Everything was ready and in order, the *blech* was set up, the house was sparkling. The Rav refused to keep the radio near the Shabbos table, so it had been placed in one of the back rooms, on the floor under a pillow. The Rebbetzin had voiced her concern that they wouldn't be able to hear it, but her husband stood his ground. "Faygie, I won't let this thing interfere with Shabbos. We're going to keep it on low and use earphones."

"But what if there's an attack?"

"*Got vet helfen*, we are not on the ground floor, Faygie, and gas is heavy. It sinks."

Finally, they agreed on a compromise. The Rebbetzin plugged earphones into the radio. This would let them listen in to emergency broadcasts if necessary without having to hear the constant drone of the radio disturbing their Shabbos.

With the radio set up at the last minute, the Rebbetzin stood weak-kneed at the door as her husband stepped out to leave for *shul*. This could be it, she thought. G-d forbid, we might never see each other again.

"Goodbye, Faygie," the Rav said.

"Hershel, where is your gas mask? Aren't you taking it to shul? Wolfson's son said there might be an attack."

"Faygie, it is not appropriate. *Es past nisht* for Shabbos!"

They both stood there, wondering if these might be their last moments on earth together.

"Hershel," she pleaded, "forgive me for anything I ever did that wasn't right by you."

He answered, "Faygie, please forgive me, too."

Then the Rav stepped out of the house. He turned back to his wife and they gave each other a victory sign despite their growing fear. The Rav went off to *shul* and the Rebbetzin lit the candles and ran into the sealed room where she sat on the bed waiting for the attack. Five minutes passed and nothing happened. Another five minutes, still nothing. She decided to *daven Kabbalas Shabbos*.

Still no attack.

She went across the hall to her neighbor's apartment, where she enjoyed a somewhat tense visit. Everything was still quiet.

The evening passed without a siren, yet the Rebbetzin's nerves were on edge. The quiet lasted until five o'clock in the morning — when the alert shattered the Shabbos early-morning air.

The attack passed without fanfare. But by the time it was over, it was almost seven in the morning. The Rav and the Rebbetzin decided to go to *shul*. They don't carry out of doors on Shabbos, so they left their masks at home.

At 20 minutes after seven the Rebbetzin was sitting in *shul* when she heard a siren. The men were downstairs *davening* and she was in the women's section with three other women. All four of them ran outside. She stopped by the entrance to the men's section to open the door so they could hear the siren. She was worried about her husband because he didn't have a gas mask. The men were *davening* with fervor. She thought that once she opened the door, they would hear the siren and run home. What she didn't know (until after it was all over) was that the Rav would not let them leave.

The Rebbetzin ran home through the deserted streets in total panic. She rushed into the sealed room and put on the radio earphones just in time to hear the announcer declare: "*Gaz b'chol ha'aretz* — there's gas all over the country." She froze. Then panic set in.

The combination of lack of sleep, Wolfson's *erev Shabbos* telephone call, and the terror of the siren had put the Rebbetzin's nervous system on overload. When she heard "*gaz b'chol ha'aretz,*" she forgot that this was simply the tail end of the standard instruction to everyone in the country to put on their gas masks ("put on your *maseichot gaz b'chol ha'aretz*"). Now, when she put on her gas mask she made up her mind to keep it on no matter what, until her husband returned from *shul*. But the minutes dragged on with no sign of his return.

Then it hit her. "What kind of a *meshugane* am I?" she said to herself. "I can't sit here in safety when my husband and others in *shul* are without their gas masks! It's *pikuach nefesh,* life threatening," she decided. "Saving a life is more important — I can't sit here doing nothing."

With determination, she put on her big black plastic raincoat and boots, as protection against gas and chemicals, and adjusted the cloth *tichel* (head-kerchief) she wore under her gas mask. Then she took Hershel's mask in hand, grabbed the pail of baking soda and water, and ran to *shul* on her mission of mercy.

The first sight to greet her eyes as she stepped into the street was an army patrol car with two soldiers wearing gas masks. They tried to stop her, indicating strongly that she should get back inside, since civilians are not supposed to be out on the streets during an attack. She motioned to them that she was going to the *shul*. With their protective gear, they looked like they were from another planet. For their part, they didn't quite know what to make of the hysterical lady in a gas mask carrying a bucket and motioning frantically, but they finally let her go.

When she arrived in *shul* it was deadly quiet. As she went to find her husband she wondered if perhaps he had made his way home already, or was in the *shul's* sealed room. But then she realized with a start that the *shul* had no radio, so they probably didn't even know there was an attack! She must warn them.

"*Gaz b'chol ha'aretz!!*" she screamed. And, banging the heels of her boots against the marble steps, she made her way up the stairs to the main entrance.

A latecomer to services ran up the steps past her, also heading for the double doors of the main entrance. He thought she was out of her mind. Once he got inside, he waited for the Rav to finish his *Shemoneh Esrei* and then said, "There's a crazy woman in a gas mask outside screaming '*gaz b'chol ha'aretz.*' The Rav stepped outside just as the Rebbetzin was nearing the top step in front of the entrance to the *shul*. At first glance, he made no connection between this creature from outer space and his wife. Then he looked again.

"Faygie," he said, "take that silly thing off your face and go home!"

"Hershel," she exclaimed with relief, "I'm so happy you are alive. They said *gaz b'chol ha'aretz!*"

"Faygie, don't believe everything they say. You can't believe everything you hear on the radio. It's Shabbos and there's a *chasan* (groom) in *shul* today. We don't want to ruin his *aufruf*. Now calm down and go home. And remember, we also have a *bris* (circumcision) to go to after *davening!*"

The Rebbetzin thought she was losing her mind. A minute ago she was sure she would find her husband lying on the *shul* floor, dying of gas poisoning, G-d forbid, and now he was casually reminding her of a *bris*. She wanted to answer him, but she couldn't take off the gas mask because she was afraid it would pull off her *tichel*. She pointed to her head and waved good-bye, then made her way home with her mask on, the bucket and her husband's gas mask in hand. She went back into her sealed room, picked up her *siddur* and glasses, and finished *davening,* gas mask and all. It wasn't long before she heard the all-clear signal. With a sigh of relief, she took off her mask, put on her wig, and ran back to *shul* for the *aufruf.*

After *shul*, the Rav and the Rebbetzin rushed to the *bris.* As they walked home from the *bris*, the Rav said, "Faygie, why did you go home? Don't you know that the safest place to be is in the *shul?*"

"Hershel," she sighed, "why didn't you tell me that *before* the air raid? You have to tell me these things or else I don't know them. But why didn't you let anyone leave *shul?*"

"Look, the *aufruf* was a certainty. *B'ezras Hashem*, it should be a good mazel for the *chasan* and *kallah* (bride). Why should I let his feelings be hurt and his *simchah* be disturbed because of a siren? There was only a very small chance of anything happening, and don't forget, we were up there on the third floor, and gas sinks, remember? Besides, the safest place is in *shul*. That we know for sure."

Then the Rav added, with a big smile on his face, "There is one other thing that the whole community now knows for sure."

"What is that, Hershel?"

"How much the Rebbetzin cares for the Rav!"

No Berachah on the Money

Many people who live in Eretz Yisrael share a common bond financially which might be called: "It never works out on paper but you always get by somehow." Time and again the story will be told of how a bill was due and right on that very day a check came in the mail, money owed was repaid, or a relative arrived bearing a cash gift. Somehow, even if it is at the last minute, those of us fortunate to live in the Holy Land get by. Like the manna in the desert, money matters can help us develop our faith and trust. Instead of manna from heaven, sometimes it feels as though we are awaiting money from heaven!

Here is a story of a couple responding to financial surprises with dignity, mutual respect and appropriate self-examination.

Shani stared in disbelief at the special-delivery letter she was holding in her hand. How could she and her husband owe 14,000 shekels in back taxes? With interest, no less! It just didn't make sense. There must be some mistake. They had an excellent accountant and the audit had gone smoothly. What could have gone wrong?

Shani decided to wait and not to disturb her husband with the letter. After all, it was still the beginning of the week, a full month and a half before the tax deadline. Their accountant had plenty of time to handle it.

Shani had learned over the years that there was much more to communication than words alone. Communication was voice tone, and also timing. It would be much easier to tell her husband about the bill if she could also present him with some concrete idea of how to pay it. It would be a shame to disturb his concentration in learning with a mere money matter.

Bernie spent at least half the day in the *beis midrash*, devoting afternoons and early evenings to his real estate business. Actually, he and Shani shared the work, but most of the time, he was the one to take potential buyers around to show them apartments. With five young children, it was nearly impossible for Shani to cover that area.

In the beginning, they had gone through some very rough financial times. In the last few years, though, the business had grown and earned a good reputation. Considering the fact that she did not have close family nearby, it was a blessing for Shani that her husband worked at home. Now her worry was that this bill would unsettle the harmonious balance they had achieved.

Her first move was to call their accountant. Then she faxed him the bill, as he suggested. She hid the threatening piece of paper at the bottom of the "pending" drawer. Bernie never got to that drawer; it was her bimonthly assignment to plow through it.

"*Baruch Hashem,* it's only money," she reminded herself, thinking back to the class she had attended the previous week. The Rabbi had said: "Money problems are the best kinds of problems to have, a fact we often forget. But when you think about all the different kinds of things that can go wrong in life, you soon realize that money problems are a *berachah*."

"*Baruch Hashem,* it's only money," she repeated to herself.

That afternoon over lunch, Shani's husband told her a story from the Gemara about how some of the Sages in

Babylon didn't even have time to sign promissory notes, they were so immersed in their learning. "So I really want to thank you," he concluded, "for taking care of all these details and freeing me to learn in the morning."

Shani sat across the table, smiling. *If you only knew the "detail" that was sitting in the drawer right now!* she thought. All she said, though, was, "You're welcome. I appreciate your acknowledgment. Details were never my strong point, but sooner or later we grow up."

As the week passed, Shani gave very little thought to the letter in the drawer. She hopefully awaited the accountant's call, while in the meantime making a list of free-loan funds she could call to borrow the money if necessary. Streamlining the budget was out of the question. As it was, during the week they lived frugally.

On Friday morning, at the end of the week, as Shani was peeling carrots, the phone rang. It was Audrey, their tenant. Ten years ago Shani and her husband had used their new immigrant rights to buy a tiny apartment in Jerusalem because she had pleaded, "Please, I'd rather live in a closet in Yerushalayim than a mansion anywhere else."

As their family grew and the business expanded they were able to move to a four-bedroom apartment with a small backyard and garden and rent out their "closet."

"Hello, Shani," said the voice on the other end of the line, "this is Audrey. I just wanted to let you know that my mortgage came through and I'm moving in four weeks. I'll call to set a time to settle up."

"That's wonderful, Audrey. I wish you lots of luck in your new home."

Shani hung up the phone with a sigh of relief. "She's really moving," she said to herself. "We have four weeks to find a new tenant."

Shani felt sad as she thought about the *chillul Shabbos* that had taken place in their little apartment over the past year. In renting to Audrey, who was not religious, she had let her heart be swayed by the woman's plight as a single parent seemingly desperate for a place to live. "I want to settle this today," Audrey had said at the time, "and move in Sunday. I'm all alone, with three children."

"One thing's for sure," Shani thought to herself now, "I will never make that mistake again, doing business after midday on Friday. I have regretted signing that contract all year."

No sooner had she hung up the phone, than her husband Bernie walked into the kitchen for a cup of coffee. Shani filled him in on Audrey's phone call, adding, "We have to make sure our next tenant is *shomer Shabbos*."

"If we can find a *shomer Shabbos* person for that area, Shani."

"Well, if we can't, I would like to ask our Rabbi if we should sell that place and instead buy a small apartment in a more *frum* neighborhood." She could see her husband's facial muscles tighten at the suggestion of taking on more debt.

"Let's wait until I find out about the inheritance, okay?" Bernie poured milk into his coffee and carried the mug towards his office.

"Sure." She didn't want him to worry. But, at the same time, she felt a need for them to take some concrete step to increase their honor of Shabbos. "Today on *erev Shabbos*, let's try to make sure we stop work at midday."

"Don't worry," Bernie laughed, "I'll be more than happy to stop exactly on time."

Bernie went into his office and Shani returned to the kitchen. A few minutes later, the doorbell rang. It was

Bernie who got there first. The mailman handed him a real estate journal and a registered letter and asked him to sign for it. Bernie slit open the official-looking envelope from the tax department with a sinking feeling. His eyes ran quickly over the computer printout down to the "total amount due" box outlined in thick black at the bottom.

"What?!" he exclaimed in a hushed tone. "This must be a mistake. We have a good accountant and the audit came out fine. How could I possibly owe 10,000 shekels?"

Bernie quickly folded the letter and put it under the pile of papers in the legal drawer. Shani never went near that drawer; legalese was not one of her strengths. It wasn't his either, but it was part of the business so he'd had to learn it.

"Why should I show this to her *erev Shabbos*? There's nothing we can do about it today and besides, the accountant has to investigate. The payment deadline is a month and a half away, so why should I upset my wife and give Satan business?" Bernie mused to himself. "I'll wait a couple of weeks, and after the accountant lets me know the results of his inquiry, we'll sit down together and figure out how to arrange for payment."

"Who was that, Bernie?" Shani called out from the kitchen.

"Just the mailman."

"What did he want?"

"He wanted to do a *chesed* and bring me the copy of the real estate journal that he had mistakenly delivered to our neighbors." The mailman *had* brought him the journal, and Shani didn't have to know about the bill. Why should her Shabbos be ruined with worry? On Sunday he would fax it to the accountant, and besides, *baruch Hashem* it was only money!

Early Sunday morning, Bernie faxed the bill to his accountant and left a message with the secretary asking him to get in touch at his earliest convenience. The rest of the morning went well. He filed the bill in a mental compartment labeled "minor problems." As he walked up the steps to his *kollel* he renewed his determination not to allow the matter to distract him from his learning. "It's a test," he told himself.

That day, as Bernie and Shani were sitting and eating lunch, the phone rang. Their usual rule was that mealtimes were not to be disturbed, but this time they both jumped up to answer.

Bernie took the call in the living room. It was the accountant. "I'm really sorry, Bernie. The audit they did covered the past five years, and it turns out that some of the deductions I took for you didn't pass."

"What do you mean they didn't pass?"

"Well, for example, you work at home and I claimed 40 percent of your house as business property. They decided to allow only 25 percent. I have no recourse on things like that — it all depends on who reviews the file and his mood that day. They say it's a law that's on the books, but in my experience it's just a matter of luck.

"I have a meeting scheduled in a week and a half to see if I can do something about this interest penalty. I'll get back to you after I see what they have to say. By the way, please pass the information on to your wife because she already called about it last Monday."

Bernie had to unclench his fist to put the receiver down. He thought fast. Obviously, Shani knew about this already. It was time for them to talk about it together. He walked back into the kitchen.

The scene that met his eyes was a heartwarming one:

Shani was feeding mashed carrots to their one-year-old son Chananel, who was gleefully mashing them all over his face, hair and bib. Bernie felt a wave of gratitude wash over him. "Thank G‑d it's only money," he thought. "It's a test."

"Who called, Bernie?" his wife asked lightly.

"Just a business call," he said, stalling for time. "Would you like to hear a little about what I was learning today?"

"Of course," she said as she wiped carrots off Chananel's face.

"Well, the Gemara was talking about a Tanna who was being harassed. He had it in his power to take revenge and inform on this person. He wrote his Rebbe a letter asking what to do. His Rebbe sent him back a letter quoting verse seven from *Tehillim* 37, which says, 'Wait silently for the salvation of Hashem and wait longingly for Him; be patient with G‑d, He will take care of your enemies; He will fell your enemies.' Most of the time we don't understand how Hashem runs the world, but one thing we do know — He is always directly involved in every detail of our lives."

Shani had a funny feeling that her husband was talking about the bill.

"Bernie, did you go looking for anything in my drawer?"

"No, why?"

"Well, why are you telling me about details?"

"First we make a *l'chaim*."

"Who are we making a *l'chaim* for?"

"To the Israel tax authorities!"

"Bernie, are you feeling okay?"

"The world is a strange place, Shani. We must be silent and Hashem will fix it." He paused and then said quietly, "I got a bill *erev Shabbos* from the audit."

"You got a bill on Friday? But I got that bill on Monday!"

"You got a bill on Monday? Did you sign for it? Why would they send us another copy?" Shani ran to her pending drawer. Bernie ran to his legal drawer. They compared bills. Bernie's Hebrew was better than hers.

"It's not the same bill, Shani. It's two bills for five years back taxes! We owe over 24,000 shekels in back taxes."

"What are we going to do?"

"Well, my inheritance money should be coming in soon. That's how we'll pay it. We have no other choice."

Shani kept quiet but she couldn't get over the irony of the situation. Her father-in-law was a Holocaust survivor. He had been receiving reparations from the Germans for many years. Now most of that money, instead of going to help his son and family build their home in *Eretz Yisrael,* would be going to the tax authorities.

Shani spent the rest of the day feeling bitter. She did make one positive decision: not to talk about it except with people she knew who might be able to give her some good advice. Otherwise, silence.

One particular friend whose husband was also an independent businessman seemed a possible source of information.

"Taxes?" Her friend Simi laughed. "My husband can't wait for *Mashiach* so he can take the tax authorities to a *beis din*! Listen, Shani, *Eretz Yisrael* is acquired through suffering. The year we got audited, we also had a very expensive piece of building equipment stolen."

"What did you do?"

"We made a *l'chaim*," Simi answered, dead serious. "If you have your health and a place to live and food to feed your family, you are the wealthiest person in the world. Here especially, the *hasghachah pratis* is so easy to see. You feel it so clearly. We can't even imagine what an incredible *chesed* was done for us."

"But Simi, how much did you have to pay?"

"Ten thousand dollars," came the answer.

Shani was shocked. "How did you pay it?"

"Every which way," laughed Simi. "And we're still paying it off. Now things are even tighter because we have to start borrowing for the wedding. But we thank G-d that we have only happy events to plan for."

Shani always knew she had a good friend in Simi.

"By the way," Shani remembered, "our little apartment is empty. If you know of anyone looking for a place could you please keep it in mind?"

"Sure."

Shani got busy trying to rent the apartment, which was in a religiously mixed neighborhood and very centrally located. Even though she received many calls, all were from non-religious people and Shani stood firm in her resolve to rent only to *shomer Shabbos* tenants.

Finally, she decided to go to the apartment and speak with other people who lived in the same building. Perhaps they would know of someone who wanted to rent in the area.

As she was inspecting the recent paint job and trying to convince Chananel to stay in his carriage, a neighbor she had never seen before came upstairs and introduced herself. It was evident that the woman was part of the religious segment of the neighborhood.

"Shalom," said the woman pleasantly, "my name is Esther. Please forgive me for saying this, but no *berachah* will ever come from your rent money unless your tenant is *shomer Shabbos*. For a whole year I suffered the smell of cigarette smoke, food cooking, and the sound of music blaring from this apartment on *Shabbos kodesh*."

Shani turned white.

"Are you all right? Let me give you a glass of water," said Esther in concern.

"No, I'm okay — I just feel so terrible about what you told me. I didn't know you lived upstairs. I thought most of the people in this building weren't religious."

"I've been here now for over five years. The neighborhood is changing for the better. Besides, what are you calling not religious? Just because a man doesn't go with a long coat that makes him non-religious? This is Jerusalem. Shabbos is Shabbos."

"I'm so sorry, Esther. I also want a *shomer Shabbos* tenant. I made a very big mistake with the last one."

As she rode home on the bus, Shani kept hearing Esther's voice, "No *berachah* will ever come from your rent money unless your tenant is *shomer Shabbos.*"

Shani felt deep remorse that her hasty lack of consideration had caused people in the building a year's worth of aggravation. She had a strong hunch that there was a connection between the recent tax bill and their renting to a non-*shomer Shabbos* tenant.

As soon as she arrived home, she went straight for the calculator and totaled up the rent money for the year. Then she totaled up the audit bills and changed both amounts into dollars. The two sums matched — almost to the penny!

"Be silent. Hashem will fight your enemies." Wasn't that what the verse in *Tehillim* said?

Verse seven. The seventh day! Shabbos!

A month and a half went by and the apartment was still not rented. Shani could see that her husband was growing increasingly uneasy about the loss of rental income. One morning she received a call from a young couple interested in renting the apartment. Shani's heart sank, though, when she realized they were not observant. She told them she would discuss it with her husband and get back to them.

"There is only one thing for us to do at this point," he said. "I'm going to call Rabbi Taylor and ask his advice."

Shani listened as her husband described the situation to the Rabbi. She flashed back to the moment she signed the contract with Audrey and the queasy feeling that followed telling her she had made a big mistake. "Please, Hashem," she murmured, "if it's Your will, let the apartment be rented this week to a *shomer Shabbos* tenant."

Bernie hung up the phone with a smile. "The Rav gave a *berachah* that the apartment should be rented this week! He also said to rent to a person who is *shomer Shabbos* and that only good things will come from it even if we have to wait a bit more."

Shani breathed a sigh of relief. That very afternoon Shani got a call from a lovely young *shomer Shabbos* couple.

"My husband can take you to see the apartment at seven o'clock tonight." She took care of the details and hoped that this would be it.

At 8:30, just as she was finishing the bedtime routine, Shani heard Bernie and the couple, Avi and Sarah, walk in. Bernie opened the door to the children's room and whispered, "They want to sign now, Shani. The Rav's *berachah* was fulfilled."

Later that evening, Bernie said to his wife, "Let's hope this marks a new beginning. By the way, Rabbi Taylor said it would be good for us to work on really honoring Shabbos and making it very beautiful, so here, take this money and buy something special for Shabbos."

Shani smiled. She felt a deep inner calm. She knew that Shabbos is the source of all blessing for the world. She was so grateful that now the *berachah* of Shabbos would rest on their little rented apartment and that the neighbor, Esther, would be pleased.

The next afternoon, Bernie sat at his desk with the rental money and the tax bill. "Sometimes," he said, "These things are negotiable. I'm going to meet with our accountant and see if they'll give us a reduction if we pay one large sum instead of payments."

"Sounds like it's worth trying," Shani replied. "But before you go out we just have to do one thing."

"What's that?"

"Make a *l'chaim*!"

❧ The Moon Was His Witness

The silent motivator in this story, Mrs. Roiza Chernitsky, traveled from Pinsk to New York to Jerusalem. In each place, the reverberations of her chesed are still felt today. Mrs. Chernitsky would even enter lobbies of the fancier hotels to approach the patrons in her broken English for their help with her many charity projects. To name just two, she was involved with orphans and housing new immigrants in her own home. Sunday morning was not a time for bagels and lox in the Chernitsky home because Roiza's hotel business prospered during Sunday morning breakfasts. Their home had a somewhat unusual beginning, as we shall see.

Moshe Chernitsky was the only child of divorced parents, which in the early 1800s in Russia was practically unheard of among observant Jewish families. His mother, Buba Tova, had to go out to work to support her child. As a result, there was no one at home to make sure he went to *cheder*. And as a teenager, he would even go to movies on Shabbos.

Then he met Roiza and knew he wanted to marry her. She, though, would have nothing to do with him because he wasn't observant.

At that time, Moshe faced induction into the Russian army. And everyone knew that once you were in their clutches, you were lost. The night before his physical, he went outside and looked up at the moon.

"Moon," he said, "you be my witness. If the *Ribbono shel Olam* saves me from the Russian army, I promise I will become *shomer Shabbos*."

Moshe had never been a smoker. In fact, smoke made him cough. Back then, when doctors heard someone cough a lot, they immediately suspected tuberculosis. Moshe thought he might be able to fool the doctors into rejecting him by staying up all night smoking to make himself cough.

In those days, a Russian cigarette consisted of about an inch and a half of cardboard tubing stuffed with cotton to serve as the filter, while the rest was tobacco rolled in paper. After a night of smoking and coughing, Moshe made his way to the induction center where he sat down and waited to be examined. The butt of a cigarette was in his lips. When they called his name, he got so frightened that he gasped and sucked in that cigarette butt which then got lodged in his throat. Now he was coughing because he was actually choking! In the examination room the doctor said immediately, "This man is sick. He's exempt."

A Russian officer standing there said, "He's sick? Look at him. He's stronger than I am. He goes in."

The doctor turned around to the officer and screamed, "Who's the doctor here? You or me? You want to be the doctor?" He ripped his stethoscope off his neck and threw it at the officer, storming past the line of waiting men.

The officer ran after the doctor and yelled, "All right, all right, he goes, but you stay."

Moshe got his exemption and, as he'd promised, became *shomer Shabbos.* Then he married Roiza!

The Rabbi Refused

As children we sometimes wonder why our parents gave us the name they did. Often the choice was not easy. Mrs. Friedman had her heart set on a certain name, but her daughter's destiny was meant to be reflected in a different signature.

Mrs. Friedman wanted to name her newborn daughter after her uncle Moshe, to whom she had been very close. She thought it would be just fine to call her Malkah, which means "queen." She loved that name and went to discuss the decision with her Rav, Rabbi Berman. He spent a lot of time with her. She tried to convince him, but it was no use. He wouldn't, he absolutely refused to allow her to use the name Malkah. He said it had to be Mashe and that was that. He was so emphatic about it that she really felt like she just didn't have a choice. She left his study a little disappointed but, thank G‑d, she had a healthy, beautiful baby and that was clearly the most important thing. That week, her daughter was named Mashe, after Mrs. Friedman's uncle.

Mashe grew up wondering why the Rabbi had been so adamant about not letting her mother name her Malkah. Malkah was such a beautiful name, what harm would there have been if her mother had had her way?

A few weeks before her wedding, she met with one of the Rabbis who was filling out the *kesubah*, to give him family details, including all the relevant Hebrew names.

That night after dinner, she mentioned casually, "By the way, Mama, I found out something very interesting today. My mother-in-law's Hebrew name is Malkah."

Mashie's mother let out a cry of understanding. "Oh! Now, after all these years, I know why Rabbi Berman refused to let me name you Malkah! In our family, we won't agree to the match if the bride has the same name as the boy's mother. But I never checked your future mother-in-law's Hebrew name." She dried her hands on her apron, put them on her daughter's head and kissed her on the forehead. "You see, what is *bashert* is *bashert*. And this was *bashert* from before you were even given your name!"

A Shiur Within a Shiur

Years ago, Mrs. Blumenthal attended a *shiur* on *shalom bayis* given by a prominent Rabbi. The lecture was part of a series in a course designed to train Orthodox women to become family counselors in the community.

"To be honest," recalls Mrs. Blumenthal these many years later, "if I hadn't taken thorough notes I don't think I would remember too much about that particular lecture. Two things, though, made such a strong impression that not only will I never forget them but they have guided me in my counseling work all these years.

"The first incident happened when the lecture was well under way. We were all intensely absorbed in listening to the Rabbi speaking when suddenly, his wife appeared in the entrance to the lecture hall. Heads turned to see who was coming late.

"The Rabbi looked up from his notes and stopped speaking. Then he smiled a big warm smile and said, '*Shalom aleichem*.' He motioned to an empty seat right down in the front row and said pleasantly, 'Please come and sit down.'

"For me," said Mrs. Blumenthal emphatically, "that was the whole *shiur*.

"The tie-in that anchored this point firmly in my mind came when the rabbi told us a story about Moshe Rabbeinu. He said that when Hashem spoke to Moshe in Midyan and told him to go to Egypt to save the Jewish people, Moshe's first response was, 'I have to ask permission from my father-in-law. He took me into his home and I am like a son to him.' Moshe was already in his 80s, the Rabbi explained, and Hashem Himself had told him to go. Why would he think he needed to ask his father-in-law's permission?

"We were all curious to hear the answer to this perfectly logical question that none of us had ever thought of before, and were sure it would have relevance to the subject we were there to learn. We weren't disappointed. 'This comes to teach us,' said the Rabbi, 'that treating another person with *derech eretz* takes precedence over the redemption of the whole Jewish people!'"

Off with the Old, On with the New

Mrs. Horowitz was known for being a woman of action. No matter how minor — or how overwhelmingly daunting — the issue might seem to be, if it needed fixing, she was in the forefront. For instance, there was the time when she stood with a group of over 100 mothers she had rounded up to demonstrate for a crossing guard at a dangerous street corner. It took only two weeks of disrupted traffic before policewoman Patty was assigned to her new corner three times a day.

Even in her marriage, when something reached a standstill and Mrs. Horowitz knew there was something she could do, she just quietly went and did it. Like the story of her husband's hat.

Mr. Horowitz was a very conservative, frugal, yet kind, man. His sole weekday hat was about five years old. The black felt was old and frayed and impossible to clean anymore. Mrs. Horowitz could no longer tolerate that hat. Their scenario went something like this: The minute Mr. Horowitz would walk in for lunch and sit down at the table, Mrs. Horowitz would say, "Hello, dear, how's your day? By the way, there's a sale on hats."

"Fine, dear, *baruch Hashem*, my day is fine, and my hat is a fine hat. I would imagine there are a lot of years left in this fabric."

Mr. Horowitz would glance at his hat, give it a fond pat, and get up to hang it on the hook beside the dining-room door. Mrs. Horowitz would purse her lips together, but say nothing. This scene repeated itself for several months, until Mrs. Horowitz came up with a plan.

One day when her husband was settled in his bath, she

grabbed his old hat and flew out the door to the haberdashery a few blocks away. "Give me one exactly like this one, please," she asked breathlessly. She paid for it, threw the old hat in the rubbish bin, and ran home.

In the meantime, Mr. Horowitz was preparing to leave for *Ma'ariv*. "Dear, can I please have my hat?" he said as he put on his overcoat.

"You can't have it," his wife said quietly and gently, with a big smile on her face. "It's gone." And very sweetly she handed him his brand new hat. "Here, you can have this instead."

Mr. Horowitz didn't say a word. Then, with the smile of a gracious loser, he declared, "I always said you were a woman of action. That's why I married you and that's why I consent to wear this hat!"

Fit for a Queen

People who have been born and raised in Jerusalem have lived through momentous times in recent Jewish history. Their daily lives are often made from events that later are written on the pages of biographies and history books. One such person is Mrs. Yona B., whom I have known for over ten years. She told me these two touching — and fascinating — stories about her parents.

"My parents instilled a very deep love for Jerusalem within us. My father, Reb Peretz, came to Jerusalem as a young man of 19 and lived in the Old City until 1947. He had a Judaica shop near Jaffa Gate which was burned down by the Arabs.

"After the war in 1948, the government gave him assistance to renovate a storefront in the area which was close to what is now the new City Hall. He was informed by the authorities that when the sign was painted, the address for the store should read 'Princess Mary 15.'

"My father came home that night, sat down at the small dinner table and said, 'It's a shame to have such a name on the front of the shop. A street in the holy city of Jerusalem to be called by the name of Princess Mary! I won't have it. We are changing the name. As of right now, the address is Rechov Shlomzion HaMalkah 15.'

"We were accustomed to Abba's fierce love for Jerusalem and all things Jewish. No one questioned how he intended, single-handedly, to implement his decision. But he did, with my mother's help.

"How did they accomplish this? First, Abba instructed the painter to paint his address — the way *he* wanted it — in bold black letters. Second, every single time a letter arrived addressed to proprietor Peretz A., 15 Princess Mary Street, he crossed it out and wrote, 'Return to sender; please use correct address.'

"My mother would faithfully bring each and every one of these letters back to the post office. And, as everyone can see, his sincere love brought about a triumphant success. Very few people walking today on Rechov Shlomzion HaMalkah know that the name was born from a heart of a fiery lover of Zion.

"But the street name incident was really a pale reflection of what stirred in Abba's heart. When he reached the age of 80, many friends and customers came to wish him mazel tov. Whenever a well-wisher asked him exactly how old he was, he would answer in all seriousness, 'Today, I am 61.'

"'Sixty-one, Reb Peretz? I thought it was closer to 80!' the friend would say.

"'My friend,' Abba would respond mournfully, 'for the 19 years Jerusalem has been in the hands of the Arabs, it hasn't been any life for me.'"

Bubbie, Tell Me Your Life

Tishah b'Av, 1492, was the final day for compliance with the edict of the Spanish expulsion. Although it was a day of national mourning, the Rabbis of that generation declared, "Take up your instruments." Thus the Jewish community marched out of their host country with the musicians at the lead. Not only did the Rabbis want to infuse the refugees with hope, they also wanted to remind them that there is only one place in the world worthy of tears being shed when we must leave there. That place is Jerusalem.

The inner command to "take up our instruments" — to begin again with renewed hope — has been the mandate of the Jew throughout exile. In recent history the most moving and remarkable examples of this have been the survivors of the Holocaust. Having faced death so many times, having endured unspeakable physical tortures and difficulties, the liberated survivor needed a different kind of courage: the courage to face his tragic experiences and move on to rebuild his life.

Mrs. Leah Kaufman epitomizes such bravery on

all fronts. Laden with nightmares of unimaginable personal horrors and losses, Mrs. Kaufman arrived in Canada, orphaned and penniless. She succeeded in rebuilding her life, becoming the proud mother of three sons, an outstanding educator, and an active member of the Jewish community. As for the past, it was locked in memory's vault, for half a century unseen and unmentioned.

There it would have remained perhaps forever, had not the urgent need to speak out arisen. Lest the world forget and be bereft of its memories, Mrs. Kaufman bravely unlocked hers. Speaking not just for herself but for the hundreds of thousands whose voices were silenced, she relived the pain of Transnistria, a place whose horrors have long gone untold because it left its few survivors mute.

Although Mrs. Kaufman speaks to us all, it was as a mother and grandmother that she first began telling future generations about a past that must never be forgotten.

One afternoon in Montreal, as Mrs. Leah Kaufman stood at her kitchen sink preparing supper, her four-year-old son ran into the house, sobbing. "Mommy, Mommy," he cried, "do you know what happened to children in the Holocaust?" He put his arms around his mother and buried his face in her apron. Suddenly, his older brother, Seth, who had been in another room doing homework, ran out, grabbed him by the shoulders, and dragged him into their bedroom.

"David," he shouted, in a voice far more adult than his six years, "never, *ever* talk to Mommy about the war or about Nazis!"

Their mother held onto the kitchen counter, unable to move. A memory flashed through her mind. It had happened a year ago, when she was in a local bookstore with Seth. There on a display counter they had encountered an oversized book with a big bold title: *Transnistria*. Seth had tugged at her hand, saying, "Mommy, isn't that where you were? Don't you want to buy the book?" She had hastily pulled him out of the store. Once outside, she bent down and looked deep into his eyes, which reflected confusion, and said, "I don't want to know. I just don't want to know."

Now, as she stood at the sink with the midafternoon sunlight slanting through the kitchen windows and the red geraniums blossoming in their white flower boxes, Mrs. Kaufman forced herself to pick up the vegetable peeler and continue her preparations for supper. Before her marriage, she had made the decision not to burden her children with her suffering. She wanted to raise them as normal, Canadian children. She would speak only one language when it came to the Holocaust: the language of silence.

Years passed since the scene in the kitchen. The boys grew, married, and raised families of their own. Pesach, 1991 found the Kaufmans at the home of Seth, now a doctor and leader in a Jewish community. A new generation of Jews was being raised, a delight to both parents and grandparents.

In the midst of the family gathering, Talia, then only eight, suddenly went over to her grandmother and said, "Bubbie, please come sit with me." Mrs. Kaufman willingly sat down on the couch next to the little granddaughter she loved so much. She was completely unprepared, though, for Talia's next words.

"Bubbie, please tell me what happened to you when you were a child."

"Just a minute, Talia," came the somewhat nervous reply, "and I'll come right back to sit with you." Mrs. Kaufman went over to her son and asked in hushed tones, "What should I do? Talia wants to know."

"Mommy," said her son, his expression suddenly serious, "please don't repeat the mistake you made with me. Tell her. Use your own judgment. I trust you."

Mrs. Kaufman went to sit on the couch, took her granddaughter's hand, and began.

"You know, Talia, we can't understand how G-d runs His world. There are many things that happened to me that are very sad. But look — here we are sitting together and I want you to know that whatever His reasons, G-d was always making incredible miracles for me and for many other people. He became our partner to help us in every way.

"My mother, your great-grandmother, was a midwife and leader. She helped anyone who came to her, Jew and non-Jew alike. When I was little, I would often be awakened by a loud banging on the window — Boom! Boom! — and shouts of, 'Domna Brachah, come quickly! We need you to deliver a baby!' My mother also knew what to do if someone was sick. She knew about herbs and special little cups to put on the skin, and leeches to pull out the diseased blood from the body. She learned all this from her mother, my grandmother, who was also a healer.

"Anyway, I remembered that one night when I was just about your age there was a banging on the window. This time, though, it wasn't an urgent call for my mother to help. No, it was an urgent call to warn our family to flee because the next day soldiers would be arriving. My mother woke me and my brothers and sisters and dressed us in layer after layer of clothing. When we left the house and made our way to the road, we saw many other families. They were all running away.

"We went to another city and took shelter in an empty house. We stayed there for a few days and prepared for Shabbos. On Shabbos, as we were sitting around the table with the wooden shutters closed, we suddenly heard a loud pounding on the shutters and the door. My mother and father told us to run and hide. My brothers and sisters and I obeyed.

"Soldiers burst in through the front door. They saw all the dishes at the table and the leader shouted, 'Where is everybody?'

"My parents said nothing.

"Then he threatened, 'If they don't come out, we will shoot you.'

"My parents called us back into the room. The soldiers lined up all seven children one by one behind each other, with the tallest standing in the back and the smallest in the front. This was so that they could shoot all of us at once using only one bullet. We said good-bye to each other. They picked up their rifles and were about to pull the trigger when suddenly their leader shouted, 'Put down your guns!'

" 'Why?'

" 'Put down your guns!' he repeated in a booming voice. To this day, I can hear his loud echoing voice inside my head. Then, in a much softer tone, he said, 'I can't kill them. This woman brought me into the world and saved my life many times. I can't kill them. Let's go.'

"That's the first time I was saved. But that was only the beginning of many difficult and terrible times. The Rumanian soldiers were brutal to the Jews and forced us to walk in the freezing winter from place to place. We had to sleep in haystacks and on the frozen ground. Many people became sick and died just from the cold.

"One of the places we stopped at was right near a bakery. The delicious smell of the freshly baked bread made our hunger pains even worse. Small as I was, I was always a fighter. I said to myself, 'There must be some way we can help ourselves.' Everyone else was lying down but I was sitting up watching the door of the bakery. I saw a little girl come out of the bakery and I called out to her in Rumanian. She was shocked. She had probably never talked to a Jewish child before. But like most children, she was curious, so she came over to me and said, 'What do you want?'

"I said, 'How old are you?' It turned out she was my age. 'Where are you going?' I asked her.

" 'To school,' she replied.

" 'Do you like school?'

" 'I hate it — because I'm not smart.'

" 'What grade are you in?' I asked.

"She told me and I told her to bring me her books. She did. I took one look at what she was learning and said to myself, *I'm going to be her tutor!* I said to her, 'Don't go to school today. Sit with me and I'll help you. Tomorrow you'll know everything.'

"She sat with me and I helped her. Then she went into her house and told her mother. Her mother was so pleased that she sent out a loaf of bread. As long as we stayed there, we had bread every day.

"My mother very much wanted us to have a chicken for Shabbos and she had an idea of how we could get one. We all had pierced ears from the time we were young. We were four sisters plus my mother, so there were five pairs of gold earrings. As we were marching, the Rumanians stood on the sidelines trading things. My mother traded all our earrings for a chicken. She sent me with it to the *shochet*. When I brought it home, she plucked the feathers and opened it. The liver didn't look quite right to her, so she sent me back to the *shochet* who looked at the liver and told me the chicken wasn't kosher.

"By this time we were very hungry, but my mother said, 'Kinderlach, mir turren dos nisht essen — My children, we are forbidden to eat this.'

"My mother and my brothers and sisters never lived to eat chicken again.

"The weather was getting colder and colder and we were being forced to march again. I was always on the lookout for ways to survive. As we walked, I watched the faces of the Rumanian soldiers. I saw that the one who was holding onto the horse leading the wagon didn't have such a cruel face. I went up to him and said, 'What is it to you if I die?'

"He looked at me and said, 'What do you want, little girl?'

"I said, 'I want to live. Let me sit in your wagon.'

"He bent down, picked me up, wrapped me in blankets, and lifted me up onto the wagon. And that is how I survived the march. From time to time my older brother would come to check up on me and bring me news from the family and little things to eat.

"Depending on where we stopped, I sometimes slept in haystacks, hidden deep under the hay. Because of my fair skin and blonde hair, and also because I spoke Russian, I would often run away and find a Russian family in the woods. I would tell them, 'I'm a Russian child. I've lost my family and I'm very hungry,' and they would give me crusts of bread. Sometimes they would take me into their fields to let me dig up a few potatoes. Whatever it was, though, was never enough to quiet the hunger pains.

"The Ukrainian children were very, very cruel. They had a game when they caught a Jewish child. They would say, 'Jew, say *kookooroisa*.' In their language that means corn. To say it, you have to know how to roll the 'r' properly. *Baruch Hashem* I passed that test many times.

"One by one my brothers and sisters died. My mother and I were left alone, until finally, one cold and bitter day, she too, died, and I was left on my own.

"I decided to try to make my way to Mogilov where I hoped to find relatives. I walked for months, all alone, fending for myself. One day, I came upon a little cafe owned by a woman. I asked her for some food, which she promised to give me if I would be willing to wash dishes in return. I agreed, and she sent me to the pump in the yard with the dirty dishes. I did the best I could, and brought the dishes inside. She said, 'Do the other side.' And she sent me back. That's how I got my lesson in how to wash dishes! Once she realized that I could be trusted, she let me help her every day.

"One day, she came to me and said, 'How would you like to come home and sleep in my house?' That was an unbelievable offer! I replied without hesitation, 'I would like that very much!'

"The first night I was there I had a very frightening dream and I screamed in my sleep in Yiddish. The woman woke me up and said, 'Lydia' — that's what I called myself because Lydia was close to Leah — 'why did you scream that way in a language I couldn't understand?'

"I told her the truth, that I was Jewish, and she said, 'Your secret is safe with me. Just don't tell another soul.' From that day on, I was always with her.

"One day, a group of German soldiers came into the restaurant and after they ate, they ransacked the place, breaking dishes and smashing furniture. The owner was hysterical and I was terrified. When we had calmed down, I said to her, 'Madame Bakouska, they were planning it!'

"She asked me, 'How do you know?'

"I told her, 'I understood what they said to each other. They didn't want to pay, so they planned the whole thing.'

"She started laughing so hard I though she had lost her mind. I asked her, 'What's wrong?'

"She hugged and kissed me and said, 'Lydia, you will never have to worry again. You will be my child.' We made a secret signal between us so that I could tell her whenever I overheard the Germans planning to do damage. She would then cross the street and bring back an equal number of Ukranian soldiers. When the Germans saw the soldiers, they would pay their bill and leave. Her business prospered and my situation was a good one.

"Suddenly, things changed. On the corner, next to the cafe, was a drug store. One day the druggist stumbled into the cafe drunk and said, 'You're doing well because she's a Jew' — he pointed to me — 'and she understands what they're saying.' From that day on we were on the alert. But what happened next was much worse than I ever expected.

"One day two Jewish kapos came into the restaurant. They were working for the enemy. When they found out I was a Jewish child, they kidnapped me and put me on a train bound for the Piciora concentration camp. I was in shock! How could fellow Jews do that to me?

"When I arrived at the camp I went into the barracks and took stock of the situation. I decided then and there that I had to escape. Everyone there looked near death. It was no place for me. I walked outside and looked around. Near the main gate was a little bush. I lay down near the bush. I was watching the guard and the guard was watching me. After a few days under the bush, a moment came when the gates were open and the eyes of the guard were on other things. I picked myself up and walked straight out. I said to myself, 'If you survive, you must remember this day.'

"Then I started my journey all over again, back to the town with the cafe, and eventually, after the war, to Canada."

Mrs. Kaufman had been holding Talia's hand with both of her own. She looked at her granddaughter's face and could see the questions and the sadness in her eyes.

"Talia, I'm going to tell you one more thing, and then it's enough for this visit, okay?"

Tali nodded her head as her grandmother continued.

"After the war, when I was liberated, I became an apprentice to a dressmaker. But it turned out she wasn't interested in teaching me anything about a needle and thread. What she really needed was someone to stand in line for food and provisions because we were under the Russian occupation.

"One day, when I was in the backyard beating the dust out of a carpet, a man came up to me and said, 'Are you Leah?'

" 'Yes,' I answered.

" 'I'm your brother!'

"He took me away from that house and helped me get into an orphanage that was in the brand-new wing of a hospital complex. It was a special place for children who were staying in Bucharest, waiting to go by boat to *Eretz Yisrael*. We waited there a few months. The very night before I was scheduled to leave for Israel, I had severe stomach pains. The doctors discovered that my appendix had burst. I was taken to the hospital in a coma. It was one of the miracles Hashem did for me that the orphanage was located in a wing of the hospital so they were able to get me there so quickly. The chief surgeon, though, said I was beyond surgery. But an orthopedic surgeon who was present said, 'You have given up on her. I would like a try,' and he operated on me. Remember, this was in the days before they had penicillin. Even today, a burst appendix is very dangerous.

"Well, this doctor put tubes inside to drain out the infection, and although I was in a coma for a whole month, I recovered. But Talia, I want you to know that the ship that left for *Eretz Yisrael* never made it there. It was struck by a torpedo. To this day, no one knows who did it, whether the Russians, the Germans, or the British. But because I was very, very sick, I wasn't on that ship. My burst appendix saved my life!

"So you see, Talia," Mrs. Kaufman concluded, "everything I was given, was given to me for a purpose. My gift of speaking many languages, my ability to quickly read people's faces and understand them, even my illness — all were part of the miracles that Hashem did to save me."

Mrs. Kaufman rose from the couch and Talia ran off to play. For the rest of the day, Mrs. Kaufman kept asking herself, "Did I do the right thing? Did I tell her too much?" She kept a close watch on her granddaughter and the next day, had her answer when Talia came over to her and said, "Bubbie, I have to talk to you."

"Okay, honey. Here I am. What do you want to say?"

"Bubbie," Talia began, "the day you die, it's gonna rain very hard." She spoke emphatically, her face serious.

"Talia, why is it going to rain so hard?"

"Because all the angels Hashem had sent to be your partners till now are going to cry so hard because they won't be able to watch over you anymore."

It is said in the name of the Chazon Ish: For those who went through the devastating Holocaust and lost their belief, we can say nothing. For those who went through it and held onto their belief, we must stand up in awe.

Epilogue: Bread upon the Waters

> *"Cast your bread upon the waters,*
> *for after many days you will find it"*
> *(Ecclesiastes 2:1).*

One day when my husband walked into *kollel*, a colleague walked up to him and handed him a piece of paper with a telephone number on it. "There's an Eliezer Medwed in Kiryat Sefer. Why not give him a call? Maybe you're related."

My husband answered, "Thanks, but I don't think we're related since I know all the family I have here in Israel."

"You never know," said the man with a smile.

When my husband told me about the incident over lunch, my curiosity was aroused. "Call, maybe he's a relative."

"It's highly unlikely," he answered, "The family was so fragmented after the war. We left Detroit when I was four and I hardly remember anything."

"That's all right," I persisted, "just call anyway."

A few hours later, I asked again. "Did you call yet? Please call, I'm so curious. Maybe we have family here!"

A few minutes later my husband picked up the phone. "Hello, this is Zalman Medwed. Someone gave me your name and suggested that we might be related. Where are you from originally? Really? Detroit? That's where my family lived before we moved to New York."

I stood there listening to my husband's end of the conversation like a detective waiting for clues. Soon afterwards I heard, "Aunt Ida? Uncle Pete? That big dog that used to jump all over? He was your Zeidie? He was my Zeidie's brother! But my Zeidie was martyred in the war. I never saw him. So you know details. I never knew any details."

It turned out that because Eliezer knew his Zeidie and Zeidie Pete lived till the age of 89 (tradition has it that this was due to the *l'chaim* he drank every day), Eliezer knew parts of the family history that we thought were lost.

We were especially interested in finding out to what *chassidus* the family had adhered. We knew that before the communists took over in Russia, my husband's family had been *chassidim* but we didn't know which sect they had belonged to, and no one else in the immediate family did either. My husband's father lost his family in the war and rarely, if ever, spoke about those difficult times except to say he had been placed in an orphanage as a child, and that his father had taught *talmidim*.

Now, as I continued listening to my husband's end of the conversation with our newly found relative, my heart filled with joy.

"It was Karlin?" I heard my husband say. "Are you sure? No kidding. Well, let me ask my wife when we can come out to see you and until then, we'll keep in touch."

When we met our cousin and his family for the first time, he filled us in on some details of our family history: "There were four brothers, all *chassidim* except for Zeidie Pete. He used to tell me that he was the rebel of the family. If his brothers had been Litvaks, he would have been a *chassid*! Their father was also a Karliner, so it was in the family for at least two or three generations."

My husband began making inquiries about the Karliner community and discovered it was known for its special warmth, friendliness and hospitality. We were invited to the home of Karliner chassidim — a young family with three small children; the husband was American, the wife, Israeli.

The truth is, the thought of spending a Shabbos away

from home did not appeal to me. I don't like to travel and I love being home for Shabbos. Also, I was concerned that we wouldn't be able to communicate easily with our hosts, which would add to the sense of discomfort. My Hebrew was still very elementary, and my Yiddish non-existent. Yet the knowledge that a wife should follow her husband's path — plus a small measure of curiosity at spending a Shabbos in Meah Shearim — got me packing.

Being in that neighborhood on Shabbos is always colorful and enchanting, and we found *davening* with the Karliners a unique and awe-inspiring experience. At the Shabbos table, we soon found ourselves relaxing in the warm family atmosphere. The talk turned to family and my husband asked our host where he was from.

"I was born in America, but we have had family in *Eretz Yisrael* for over 200 years."

"Really!" exclaimed my husband. "Where did they live?"

"In Teveryah. My grandfather headed a *kollel* there. His name was Perlman."

My husband turned to me in excited amazement. "Did you hear that? His grandfather had a *kollel* in Teveryah and his name was Perlman. Maybe he's the Rabbi your grandmother sent *tzedakah* money to?"

"Maybe ..." my voice trailed off. "But I doubt it. After all, it's such a common name."

Shabbos passed all too quickly, as usual. On Sunday I called my mother. "Ma, didn't you save some of Bubbie's letters and documents?"

"Yes, sweetheart, I did, because I felt they were worth saving; especially that letter from Rabbi Perlman, of blessed memory. He was the Rabbi in Teveryah. Remember that story I told you about the charity money during the war that Bubbie sent to him? Of all my mother's papers, that is the letter I treasure the most because it contains the blessings of a *tzaddik*."

"Mama, would it be possible to send me a copy of that letter?"

"Of course — but it's in a complicated Yiddish so you'll need a translator."

The letter arrived the following week. My mother had even photocopied the outside of the aerogram so I could see how it looked. As I looked at the address, Mrs. F. Davis, 49 Allendale St, Springfield, Massachusetts, United States, America, I thought to myself, "Some people inherit china and silver from their grandmothers but who knows what unseen riches I am holding in my hands right now."

It took a while to get the letter translated. It was a firsthand account of the terrible hunger and lack of provisions people in Israel were suffering then. The date is too blurred to read clearly:

> Dear Devoted Sister and Friend, Feige Chaya Davis and your dear children,
>
> I received your letter as well as the three food packages. Thank you very much for this relief aid which sustains us. I immediately replied to confirm the receipt of the packages. But the situation here is one I never before experienced. I am very disturbed by the predicament and I think that the whole world is aware of what is going on in *Eretz Yisrael*. The hunger persists and the cost of living is extremely high here. One is unable to acquire basic needs such as medicine. My mind is so occupied with all of this that I can't do anything.
>
> As far as sending further aid, the best thing would be if you could send food packages, not dry milk

powder but liquid milk in cans. Also coffee, tea, sardines, matzos, fruit, etc.

I want to send warm regards to my wonderful friends who are taking part in this great mitzvah of *pikuach nefesh*. May Hashem *Yisbarach* repay you with everything good and bless you with a lot of success and much *nachas* from your dear children. You should have everything good in this world and in the World to Come in *Gan Eden,* and your requests should be answered for the good, Amen.

My dear friend, Feige Chaya, I have much to write about but unfortunately I don't have patience. The situation is such that I am thinking of coming to America soon. But the place where I was to have stayed in Boston is no longer prepared to accommodate me as it is now owned by someone else. According to my information, there is a shortage of apartments in America too, especially for a man who wants to observe Yiddishkeit, Shabbos and kashrus. This is making me think twice about coming to America. In addition to this, I would be very lonely there in the beginning. G-d should have *rachmanus* and bring light to *Klal Yisrael* and to every individual.

You write that you have a pillow and a blanket. If you could send it over it would be very good. Also, try to send a food package every month because this is a matter of life or death. The truth is, if I could get the main necessities from my friends I would not want to go to America. But if, *chalilah*, I would not be able to receive the major necessities, then I would have to travel immediately to America without further thought because my strength is expiring from not having with what to sustain myself, may Hashem have mercy.

You can show this letter to your best friend, Rabbi Sheinkop, as well as to Rabbi Segal. They should immediately send whatever aid they can.

To Mrs. Rochel Kempner,

My dear good-hearted friend, my best thanks for your holy assistance in money via your dear mother and devoted friend, the *tzadekes* Feige Chaya. I wish you and your dear family all the best, good health, *parnasah*, a lot of *nachas* and a *refuah shleimah* to your mother-in-law Rivkah. With the best of health, awaiting a *yeshuah*.

HaRav Perlman

Weeks later I realized that we knew the Rav's first name because his official stamp was on the letter. My husband held the photocopy in his hand as he dialed the number of our Shabbos hosts. Once again I listened to the telephone conversation like a detective. It wasn't long before the answer came.

"The stamp on the letter," my husband said, "says HaRav Chaim Yehudah Perlman, Teveryah, Palestine." There was a pause, and then he turned to me and said, "That was his Zeidie!"

I felt like I was going to faint! My Bubbie in America sent charity to our Shabbos host's grandfather in Palestine in the late 1940s. We were awed at the way Hashem had guided us to this very home. I imagined my Bubbie's home as she collected and arranged the food packages. I envisioned the long mahogany dining-room table covered with the things HaRav Perlman requested: sardines, cans of milk, coffee, tea, fruit, matzos, basic medical supplies, alcohol, and of course some of Bubbie's home remedies. I can imagine her sisters and neighbors gathered well into the night to carefully pack the boxes, and Zeidie loading them into the car to take them to the post office. I can almost see in front of me the letter with the lists of names of young men who gave her *tzedakah* before they left for the army.

Our Sages tell us that charity never gets lost. The strength of simple deeds emanating from her home, done with a kind heart with no thought or expectation of repayment, was a shield for her descendants. It is a spiritual truth that Hashem "remembers *chesed* until the thousandth generation." I felt extremely grateful to have been given the privilege to see this so clearly.

I was following my husband's search for his chassidic roots and Hashem presented me with a little piece of His Divine puzzle from our own family. How the deeds of our ancestors follow us, casting an invisible protective shadow! This time it was as though Hashem took a page from the inner scroll of my Bubbie's life and put it directly into my hands. And here I was, 50 years later, reading that letter at my kitchen table in Jerusalem.

It is 12 years since that afternoon walk in the cold Jerusalem rain. We are waiting for the time, speedily in our days, when Hashem will wipe away the tears from all our faces, when the *Shechinah* will be restored in its full glory and when all of Hashem's children will come home.

Until then, we as Jewish women are links in a chain that thousands of years of *galus* have not broken. We have the strength and ability, we have been given the nobility of spirit to move forward with our own individual melodies to this verse: "How goodly are thy tents, O Yaakov, thy tabernacles, O Israel!"

"The Children of Israel built dwelling places for G-d in many places so that His Presence might rest among them: in the Wilderness, in Gilgal, in Shiloh, in Nov, Givon and Yerushalyim. Wherever His Name was mentioned, G-d came down and blessed that place. G-d said: I shall leave all of my heavenly legions and descend to dwell among Israel.

Now, though, all those dwelling places are in ruins, as is His Holy Temple where He chose to dwell. There is one dwelling place of G-d that can never be destroyed — a Jewish home. In that home, the Divine service continues uninterrupted; the Jewish family will be the source of the redemption of Israel" (*A Jew and His Home*, Eliyahu Kitov, p. 38).

This volume is part of
THE ARTSCROLL SERIES®
an ongoing project of
translations, commentaries and expositions
on Scripture, Mishnah, Talmud, Halachah,
liturgy, history, the classic Rabbinic writings,
biographies and thought.

For a brochure of current publications
visit your local Hebrew bookseller
or contact the publisher:

Mesorah Publications, ltd

4401 Second Avenue
Brooklyn, New York 11232
(718) 921-900